T0339854

Classics at Primary School

This is the first book to provide a practical toolkit, grounded in both current educational practice and pedagogical research, on teaching Latin and ancient Greek at primary school with the aim of empowering primary school age children who do not traditionally get access to Classics in education.

Taking the author's decade of experience in coordinating primary school-level Classics projects in the UK and Belgium as a starting point, this book investigates how we can move towards educational equity by teaching primary school pupils Latin or ancient Greek. Following an introduction to educational inequity and the role of Classics in this issue, readers encounter four aspects of teaching Classics at primary school which, together, improve educational equity: widening participation, transformative learning, translanguaging, and community engagement. Through reflections on the author's personal experiences, practical steps are set out in each chapter to demonstrate how these ancient languages may be taught at primary school in ways that are accessible for every pupil. Each chapter ends with a series of reflection questions to help readers consider future practices.

Classics at Primary School: A Tool for Social Justice is designed for all those engaged or interested in teaching Latin or ancient Greek at the primary school level. Both the practical and theoretical components of this book appeal to teachers as well as researchers and policy makers with a background in education and/or Classics.

Evelien Bracke currently lectures Ancient Greek Literature and Teacher Training at Ghent University (Belgium). She coordinates the *Ancient Greek – Young Heroes* project which brings ancient Greek to primary school pupils growing up in deprived circumstances, and has published widely on the topic.

Classics In and Out of the Academy: Classical Pedagogy in the Twenty-First Century
Series editors – Fiona McHardy and Nancy Rabinowitz

This series of short volumes explores the ways in which the study of antiquity can enrich the lives of diverse populations in the twenty-first century. The series covers two distinct, but interrelated topics: 1) ways in which classicists can engage new audiences within the profession by embedding inclusivity and diversity in school and university teaching practices, curricula, and assessments, and 2) the relevance of Classics to learners from the most marginalized social strata (e.g. the incarcerated, refugees, those suffering from mental illness).

Classics and Prison Education in the US
Edited by Emilio Capettini and Nancy Sorkin Rabinowitz

Classics at Primary School
A Tool for Social Justice
Evelien Bracke

Inclusive Classics
Innovative Pedagogies in Museums and Schools
Edited by Arlene Holmes-Henderson

Classics at Primary School
A Tool for Social Justice

Evelien Bracke

Routledge
Taylor & Francis Group

LONDON AND NEW YORK

First published 2023
by Routledge
4 Park Square, Milton Park, Abingdon, Oxon OX14 4RN

and by Routledge
605 Third Avenue, New York, NY 10158

Routledge is an imprint of the Taylor & Francis Group, an informa business

British Library Cataloguing-in-Publication Data
A catalogue record for this book is available from the British Library

Library of Congress Cataloging-in-Publication Data
Names: Bracke, Evelien, author.
Title: Classics at primary school : a tool for social justice / Evelien Bracke.
Description: Abingdon, Oxon ; New York, NY : Routledge, 2023. | Series: Classics in and out of the academy | Includes bibliographical references and index. |
Identifiers: LCCN 2022039273 (print) | LCCN 2022039274 (ebook) | ISBN 9781032135359 (hardback) | ISBN 9781032135397 (paperback) | ISBN 9781003229742 (ebook)
Subjects: LCSH: Classical philology—Study and teaching (Elementary) | Social justice and education.
Classification: LCC PA74 .B73 2023 (print) | LCC PA74 (ebook) | DDC 372.658044—dc23/eng/20220831
LC record available at https://lccn.loc.gov/2022039273
LC ebook record available at https://lccn.loc.gov/2022039274

ISBN: 978-1-032-13535-9 (hbk)
ISBN: 978-1-032-13539-7 (pbk)
ISBN: 978-1-003-22974-2 (ebk)

DOI: 10.4324/9781003229742

Typeset in Times New Roman
by codeMantra

The data that support the findings of this book are available from the corresponding author, Evelien Bracke, upon reasonable request.

To my son, Morgan,
the inspiration behind my projects,
who teaches me to see the light in each child

Contents

Figures

Tables

Acknowledgements

This book is the culmination of more than ten years of my experimenting with, collaborating and reflecting on, and talking and writing about, Latin and ancient Greek at primary school, first in the UK and then in Belgium. It is intense and often stressful work, and I regularly wonder why I do not choose an easier life – but then I have inspiring conversations with colleagues and teachers, or hear from pupils and students about the positive impact of the project on their lives. These exchanges keep me focused on what matters to me, which is contributing meaningfully – in my own minor way – to a more equitable world. To put names on all of these exchanges that span over a decade and a fair number of countries is impossible, and so my acknowledgements are necessarily incomplete.

First of all, my thanks go to colleagues in the College of Arts and Humanities at Swansea University where my first primary school classics project *Literacy through Classics* saw the light, to the teachers at the schools in Wales where my students taught over a period of seven years, to colleagues from other British universities I worked with on public engagement, and to the students and pupils who took part in the project. For their support of my second primary school classics project, *Ancient Greeks – Young Heroes*, my gratitude goes to colleagues in Flemish and Dutch universities (particularly my *alma mater*, Ghent University), as well as the school teachers, students, and pupils who welcomed my project with an open mind. I also wish to thank specific funding bodies for their support over the years: Classics for All, the Classical Association, the Hellenic and Roman Societies, the Welsh Government Knowledge Exchange Fund, the Leverhulme Trust, the UGent Faculty of Arts and Philosophy CWO and Greek Section, and the Alexis Liénard trust (KBS). The National Museum of Antiquities in Leiden, and colleagues and students at Leiden University, in the Netherlands offered exciting collaborative opportunities.

My understanding of Classics at primary school level has benefited from discussions and collaborations with many people, and I am profoundly grateful to them all – but three people require a special mention. First, Lorna Robinson of *The Iris Project* in Oxford was already teaching Latin in primary schools when I first had the fledgling idea, and my cooperation with her hugely influenced my approach to the concept of primary school classics. Secondly, Barbara Bell, the author of *Minimus*, was such a monumental figure in primary school classics when I started out, I was in awe of her when we met, but her compassionate support and understanding of the pitfalls of teaching Latin at primary school made a world of difference to me. Thirdly, throughout all of our meetings and joint events, Steven Hunt, Senior Teaching Associate at Cambridge, reinforced and challenged my thought processes on (primary) classics teaching in the kindest way possible. I also thank everyone who read early chapters of this book, especially Tine Scheijnen who read pretty much the entire book twice, which vastly improved it – errors remain my own. My gratitude goes to Marcia Adams and Muhilan Selvaraj at Routledge Publishers, for their professional support during the publishing process, to Fiona McHardy and Nancy Rabinowitz, the editors of the *Classics in and out of the Academy* series, and to the anonymous reviewers, for their thoughtful and constructive feedback.

I am grateful to all of my university students for their help over the years, but particularly thank the following students for allowing me to include in this book the didactic material they created while working with me on *Young Heroes*: (in alphabetical order) Sien Denduyver, Willemijn Fortuin, Lenie Himpe, Meike Rozenbrand, Corine Van den Bergh, Merel Van Nieuwerburgh, and Andrée Walravens. I also wish to thank Steven Delarue of the Ghent Education Centre for the use of a page in their 'language passport'.

Living away from Belgium for 17 years means that 'family' has come to have a broad meaning to myself and my son, Morgan. I am grateful to the 'uncies' and aunties from our wonderful international urban family who bring so much joy to our lives, but also to our 'real' families for their continued support. My final thanks go to my mum and Morgan, for their endless encouragement and patience while I was writing this book.

1 Connecting social justice and classical languages

1.1 The edge of the beginning

In September of 2010, depression hit me and I found myself standing at the edge of an abyss. Arriving at this point had been a slow process: I had left my beloved Ireland for Wales, a country I hardly knew, and had become a single parent shortly thereafter. I was struggling to make ends meet because I insisted on staying in academia in the UK after finishing my PhD, which meant working a variety of temporary part-time jobs. I also felt useless as a scholar of ancient Greek myth, unable to make a contribution to the inequality I witnessed in the world. There was one steady beacon in this void which kept pulling me back from the edge: my love for my then two-year-old son. Yet there was also a second light in the darkness – perhaps rather a shimmer – which intrigued me. I had recently learned about *The Iris Project* coordinated by Lorna Robinson, through which Oxford University students taught Latin in local primary schools. Discussions with my own students convinced me that this was a useful thing to do, and would have a positive impact on both the students and the pupils who would take part. It took a while for light to return to my life, but this shimmer of an idea was instrumental, as it brought a sense of purpose to my working life. I went on to create the *Literacy through Classics* project at Swansea University in 2011,[1] which I coordinated for seven years; during that time I brought classics[2] to thousands of children in the South Wales area with the help of hundreds of university students (the project continues, now run by Maria Oikonomou). When I moved back to Belgium (my homeland) after Brexit, I similarly designed the *Ancient Greeks – Young Heroes* project at Ghent University in 2018,[3] through which we already reached more than a thousand school pupils.

I am a private person and feel uncomfortable telling this story. However, I feel compelled to share this information since the expertise I

DOI: 10.4324/9781003229742-1

have gained over the space of a decade concerning the teaching of classics at primary school is intrinsically bound up in my own lived experience, and I feel the book is incomplete without this information. In hindsight, it is clear I was drawn to support the pupils in our target group – those from a disadvantaged background – because of my own experiences. First, as a single mother, I have come to know very well the balancing act it takes to remain on the right side of the thin line between financial security and hardship. In most countries, child poverty is disproportionately high among single-mother families,[4] and I appreciate that I am able to remain on the right side of that line because of my family's support. Secondly, when he was little, my son loved engaging with ancient Greek myths and writing the ancient Greek alphabet. It was often a lifeline for him during difficult times, which made me realize the healing potential of myth for children. Thirdly, while I know from conversations with school teachers and pupils, and university students, that my projects have been inspiring to many of them, life-changing indeed for some, they have also transformed my own life, and so I am grateful to be able to continue this work in service of others. Finally, while my academic projects with primary schools have brought me much fulfilment and joy for over a decade, they have also exposed me to harsh criticism and ugly personal attacks, sometimes to the point of exhaustion. My strategy has become to keep going while not expressing my vision too loudly, so people would focus on the results of the project, not my personal work. As I have gained more than a decade of experience and have had the privilege of seeing the impact of my projects on many of its participants, I feel I must now share my reflections. There may be aspects of this book with which you will disagree, but by starting from a place of service and love – love of learning, of our subject, of our children – I hope you, the reader, and I will be able to enter into a meaningful dialogue.

My pedagogical practice is hence intimately connected to my personal lived experience. As John Hattie (2009: 22) argues: 'the biggest effects on student learning occur when teachers become learners of their own teaching, and when students become their own teachers'. For more than a decade, I have reflected on how studying classics can empower primary school pupils to become aware of, and engage actively in, their own learning. This book gathers these reflections on my experiences as teacher and learner, and is therefore not a traditional theoretical monograph: while I do frame the personal pedagogical practice I have gathered over the past 11 years in current evidence-based theory, the book is designed as a practical toolkit, with reflection tools at the end of each chapter to guide the reader.

The following four chapters outline an approach to teaching classics at primary school by means of four guiding social justice principles with which I have experimented over the past decade. Before we explore these four aspects, I first want to explain why it is important to take a social justice approach to classics teaching at primary school, by looking at the effects of social inequity on, and its materialization in, educational access and opportunities, and where classics fits into the picture. As the teaching of classics at primary school is primarily situated in Europe and the US and data are only available for these areas, my focus will be on educational practices there. I just said this is not a theoretical monograph, but this chapter does contain a fair amount of data and theory. I have integrated this information as I consider it vital contextualization for the pedagogical practices I will explore in the following chapters.

To clarify my terminology, when I mention 'students' or 'student-teachers', I am referring to university students (who are training to become teachers). By 'pupils', I mean both primary and secondary school pupils, while 'teachers' are primary or elementary, secondary (middle and high school), or indeed university teachers.

1.2 Social inequity and education

You may have surmised from my introduction that I have lived in Belgium, Ireland, and the UK for extended periods of my life. What started as a short Erasmus exchange stay at Maynooth University in Ireland from my home university of Ghent in Belgium turned into seven years and a PhD. This led to a move to Wales (UK), where I worked at Swansea University for ten years before returning to Belgium. Awareness of social inequity came slowly to me. It was only when I moved to Wales that I started observing stark differences in affluence, for example, between the east and west of Swansea and throughout the South Wales (post-)industrial valleys. My moment of *anagnorisis* – my recognition of the lived reality of deprivation – came when I had already started the *Literacy through Classics* project and was observing a lesson taught by my students. One pupil exclaimed how much they loved baking Roman bread, but when I suggested, 'You have the recipe now, why don't you bake it again at home with your parents?', answered: 'My mammy doesn't have money for flour.' It is not that I had no knowledge of this stark poverty before, but the sudden confrontation with this ten-year-old who was acutely aware of the limited opportunities which shaped the boundaries of their life struck me deeply. Poverty often remains unseen, but has tangible consequences: not every child grows up enjoying the same opportunities, and there are stark differences between those children who grow up in affluence and opportunity, and those who grow up in abject poverty, which shape their respective futures. A brief comparison of Wales and the Flemish region (two regions I know well) will exemplify the mechanics behind this social inequity.[5]

1.2.1 Mechanics of social inequity

Poverty is not merely a lack of financial means. The United Nations Development Programme defines poverty as 'multidimensional', meaning it is calculated on the basis of three interlinked factors, namely health (nutrition and child mortality), education (years of schooling and school attendance), and standard of living (cooking fuel, sanitation, drinking water, electricity, housing, and assets).[6] Living in multidimensional poverty has tangible effects on people's lives, as they

> are deprived of opportunities to participate fully in socially valued goods, such as education, work, and housing. This situation is not a one-off event, but constitutes a long-term plight at both the material and intangible [for example financial and cognitive] level.[7]

UNICEF reveals that children are more likely to live in poverty than adults, and are 'also more vulnerable to its effects'.[8] In the Flemish region, 14% of children live in multidimensional poverty, in comparison with 10% of the population as a whole. When this figure is broken down, however, the impact of poverty is revealed to be highly skewed, since child poverty is particularly prevalent in major cities (27% in comparison with 7% in the countryside), and among children with a non-Belgian mother (32% in comparison with 6% among children with a Belgian mother). Children from single parent (34%) and unemployed families (75%) are also disproportionately at risk. It is, moreover, important to acknowledge the intersection of both factors, since children with a non-Belgian mother and/or single parent living in an urban area are disproportionately affected.[9] Children's opportunities in life are hence not determined on the basis of just *one* social factor: ethnicity, location, class, and parental marital status must be considered jointly in order to understand the factors affecting children growing up in poverty.

The Flemish example resonates with figures from Wales, where 31% of children live in poverty, though again that figure is skewed by the relative overrepresentation of certain social groups, such as children from single families (46%) or unemployed households (73%), or with a disabled parent (38%); again, there is some overlap between the three categories.[10] As you can see, in both regions, certain social groups are disproportionately affected by child poverty. These groups are similar though not exactly the same in Wales and Flanders: ethnicity is a less important indicator in Wales than in Flanders, for example, while disability features less visibly in Flemish figures. Similar statistics on levels of child poverty as well as disproportionately overrepresented groups can be found for most so-called developed countries, where UNICEF reveals on average one in seven children grows up in poverty, though even more children are considered to be 'at risk' of being affected by poverty.[11] Child poverty, moreover, does not end when children grow up. It usually becomes more pronounced at a later age, with disastrous consequences: children growing up in poverty have less access to educational and cultural opportunities, which leads to fewer employment opportunities and lower wages, weakening social relations, decreased civic and political participation, and an increased risk of (mental) health issues, abuse, and living in a high-crime area later on in life.[12] All around the globe, charity and government initiatives work hard to provide opportunities for children growing up in deprived circumstances. In spite of their efforts, the social inequity associated with child poverty persists and has a detrimental impact on children's lives; moreover, it is set to grow exponentially due to the effects of the pandemic, armed conflict, and climate change.[13]

It is important to remember that behind these abstract statistics lie stories of individual children. In the many years I have coordinated projects with primary schools, I have met children who started school not knowing how to turn the pages of a book, whose nourishment comes largely from food banks, who get bullied for wearing hand-me-downs, who suffer abuse or neglect which impacts their behaviour and grades in school. While statistics demonstrate the severity and reach of poverty, it is the lived experiences of individual children that matter. Poverty is not an identity – I avoid using terms such as 'poor' or 'deprived' children as if this is their defining epithet – but it does impact on every aspect of children's lives. Indeed, the lack of opportunities these children suffer in comparison with their more affluent peers materializes very early on in life.

1.2.2 The role of educational inequity

Education has been mentioned a number of times in the above discussion of multidimensional poverty, and the United Nations Development Programme indeed considers it one of its three defining factors.[14]

Educational deprivation is, however, not only a contributing factor of social inequity but also a tangible effect thereof. John Hattie (2009: 62) reveals that

> when [pupils] from lower SES [socio-economic status] groups start school, they have, on average, spoken about 2.5 million words, whereas those from higher groups have spoken 4.5 million words: this demonstrates a remarkable difference in what [pupils] bring to school. The lack of resources, the lower levels of involvement in teaching and schooling, the lesser facilities to realize higher expectations and encouragement, and the lack of knowledge about the language of learning may mean that [pupils] from lower SES groups start the schooling process behind others.

Since they start school at a disadvantage to their peers, pupils from a deprived socioeconomic background are more vulnerable to entering a downward spiral of decreasing aspirations during their educational trajectory.[15] Starting with lower expectations means that these pupils receive less educational support and fewer stimuli than their peers. Shaped by this definition of them by their surroundings, it is no wonder many of these children grow up with low expectations of themselves. These low expectations have a tendency to lead to less support provided not just by teachers but by children's social network, which tends to impact their grades negatively – this confirms the initial low expectations. In this way a downward spiral is activated, until those involved (not only pupils and teachers but also parents, family, the wider social circle, and society) become convinced of the lower cognitive abilities of these children, and start treating children according to this bias[16] – a disturbing example of the Golem effect, which describes how lower expectations cause the very behaviour they predict. It leaves pupils at risk of dropping out of, or scraping through, school, and starting their working life without much hope of improving their situation. This downward spiral, combined with its dire consequences for physical and mental health later in life, reveals the disadvantage at which children living in multidimensional poverty start in life, and demonstrates that interventions early on in children's lives are necessary if they are to have any opportunities to escape a life of poverty.

Social inequity does not only have an effect on the way society looks at certain pupils; it is in fact difficult to disentangle social and educational deprivation, as inequity is embedded deeply into education systems of different countries.[17] In the UK, for example, a differentiation is made between state-maintained and independent schools, with the latter only accessible for around 6% of children who are able to afford the school fees.[18] In Flanders, every school is in theory accessible for each pupil, yet in practice, there exists educational inequity primarily differentiated on the basis of ethnicity and class:[19] schools with high numbers of ethnic minority pupils, sometimes referred to as 'concentration' schools, stand in stark contrast to non-concentration schools. This educational differentiation is clearly connected to social segregation, particularly on the basis of class, ethnicity, and location. The location of the different school types indeed correlates to residential segregation: more affluent parents make more active choices regarding their children's education based on better access to information and a higher ability to travel to get to their school of choice, while children from a deprived background and/or an ethnic minority background tend to attend their local school out of necessity and lack of information. The agency of middle-class parents leads to 'social enclosure in education', as their decisions impact on the more passive choices of working-class and ethnic minority groups, which then becomes a self-fulfilling prophecy, as schools become labelled and then attract more of the same social group, leading to so-called concentration.[20] This inequity in itself does not imply, however, that the independent sector in the UK or non-concentration schools in Flanders are necessarily 'better' than the state-maintained and concentration schools. When it comes to school results, pupils in either school type are able to perform well, or badly.[21] It does mean we need to acknowledge an educational sliding scale on a continuum between schools with the most encumbered access (primarily state-maintained and 'concentration' schools) and those with the easiest access (mostly private and non-concentration schools), on the basis of 'access' as discussed above, whether to location, information, resources, or indeed finances.

Access to resources is, indeed, the one crucial differentiating factor between these school types. Both independent schools in the UK and non-concentration schools in Flanders offer more extensive resources (for example, lower pupil–teacher ratios or teachers with higher qualifications),[22] and these privileges have a significant impact on pupils' futures. I do not mean that pupils from independent or non-concentration schools will necessarily perform better than their peers in less privileged schools,[23] but rather that they encounter fewer barriers when accessing culturally valued goods, such as higher education and better employment, and are therefore more likely to attain them. When we consider the UK, a study has indeed demonstrated that the resources of private sector schools – up to three times the resources per pupil – and small pupil–teacher ratios have a direct positive impact on children's access to university and the labour market; the Sutton Trust indicates that graduates from the independent sector still have disproportionate access to high-level professions in comparison with their peers.[24] In Flanders, scores on the international PISA tests which gauge literacy and numeracy among 15-year-olds correlate more strongly than in most other countries to socioeconomic status: pupils from a higher socioeconomic status (who tend to attend non-concentration schools) generally score higher on the PISA literacy and numeracy tests than those from a lower socioeconomic status (who tend to attend 'concentration' schools).[25] The impact is clear: a disproportionately high number of pupils from 'concentration' schools drop out of school, while they also have disproportionately low access to higher education.[26]

While many state-maintained schools in the UK and 'concentration' schools in Flanders are able to grant pupils access to culturally valued goods, the deck is stacked against them as they start from a lower baseline both financially and socioeconomically than schools with more affluent pupils, in more affluent areas.[27] This implies that some children are raised and educated in prosperity and opportunity, while others – on account of factors beyond their control – grow up in deprivation and marginalization. These are extremes on a continuum of access, and many pupils attending either school type will be somewhere in the middle, but the difference between the lived experiences of children attending schools at the extremes of this educational scale is stark. In both the UK and Flanders, it is therefore clear that the socioeconomic context in which children grow up has an impact on the educational opportunities to which they have access, which in their turn have an impact on access to other highly valued goods, such as high-level employment and higher education.

'Access' is not only an issue in the UK and Flanders. Considering the reading ability of ten-year-olds in 50 countries, the 2016 PIRLS results indicate that pupils who have access to more learning resources and digital devices at home, and who attend schools in a safe area with more affluent than disadvantaged pupils, perform significantly better than their peers who lack these resources and opportunities.[28] These data tell a grim tale about mechanisms in education systems around the world, whereby privilege is extended to some while withheld from others on the basis of access to resources (whether material or immaterial). Children with access to privilege early on in life find it easier to access culturally valued commodities, such as education and then higher education and employment, later on in life. Children who grow up in deprivation early on in life and lack the same opportunities, by contrast, will find it hard to gain access to the same culturally valued goods based on merit alone.

This short discussion has explored how inequitable access to culturally valued goods, among which education – with its lifelong negative consequences for children from deprived socioeconomic backgrounds – is a systemic, not an individual's, failing. It is true that some children are able to trade their marginalized position for one of privilege. Such individuals tend to be presented as role models by proponents of meritocracy, who argue that, if anyone can do it because of their individual excellence, whoever is willing to work hard has the opportunity to excel. The uneasy truth is that children who escape their disadvantaged circumstances are exceptions, who have usually received support from *somewhere* (an engaged teacher, financial support which allowed them to access a more privileged level of education): much as we might wish, our society is not a meritocracy.[29] Barriers – some visible (such as educational structures), some invisible (such as bias) – act as gatekeepers to knowledge and power.

Systemic work is therefore needed to raise awareness of, and start to remove, these barriers and gatekeepers, in order to balance access to resources, that is, to work towards social justice. Precisely what 'social justice' work entails depends on the context to which it is applied. The UN, for example, defines social justice with an economic focus as the 'fair and compassionate distribution of the fruits of economic growth' attained through 'strong and coherent redistributive policies conceived and implemented by public agencies'.[30] However, when we consider social justice with regard to education, Ides Nicaise (2000) argues that it has to target failure of equity on both the 'demand' and 'supply' side, namely failure on the part of certain social groups not to take up certain educational provisions ('demand'), as well as failure on the part of educational policy and practice, by disadvantaging certain groups, whether through active discrimination or inaction ('supply'). In order to target both failures, Nicaise (2000: 38) argues it is imperative to use two strategies: 'those aimed at ensuring more equal opportunities (or more equal access), and those aimed at more equal treatment within education itself'. For social justice work to be effective, it must thus engage with both policy and practice by reaching out to all stakeholders. It must go beyond tokenism, beyond good intentions.[31] Awareness of this educational inequity as well as of the pathways towards social justice is key when we reflect on the study of 'classics' which has traditionally acted as one particular educational and social gatekeeper. However, that also means classics has strong potential to be applied as a tool for social justice, as I will go on to demonstrate.

1.3 Classics and social justice

In any education system, knowledge imparted to pupils is never ideologically neutral:[32] those in power indeed promote certain canonical knowledge which is presented as truth, while other knowledge is forgotten, suppressed, marginalized, or disregarded. Curriculums are designed not only to validate the knowledge deemed important by hegemonic social groups but also to transmit it further. This has a huge impact on what children learn in school, and it is in this context that the educational inequity which I just discussed – with different outcomes and diverging higher education and career opportunities for pupils growing up at the extremes of poverty and affluence – must be understood. It is impossible, first, to deny that classics has played a role in hegemonic narratives in previous centuries, and secondly, that, in education, it continues to be inaccessible to the majority of learners. Before we look at the pedagogic potential of classics as a tool for social justice, let us therefore define the space classics holds within inequitable education systems.

1.3.1 'The glory that was Greece // and the grandeur that was Rome'[33]

The study of antiquity – and particularly of the Latin and ancient Greek languages – has long been used by ruling classes as a cultural code of belonging, a corpus of knowledge which is 'claimed to possess a special authority as the repository of exemplary cultural value'.[34] This code was not established on the basis of certain objective criteria: classics is not in itself superior to other knowledge. It was rather established on the basis of specific language ideologies. The latter are 'morally and politically loaded representations of the nature, structure, and use of languages in a social world'.[35] These ideologies 'endow some linguistic features or varieties with greater value than others [...] Language ideology can turn some participants' practices into symbolic capital that brings social and economic rewards and underpins social domination [...]'.[36] Because of language ideology, throughout the past few centuries, European societies and their former colonies – and through them their different educational systems – have attributed a highly symbolic value to 'Latin', 'ancient Greek', and/or 'classics'. Ofelia García (2019: 369–70) puts it bluntly: '[E]ducation for the dominant classes included the learning of Latin, a code that was not meant to be used in real life, but simply to differentiate social classes. To be educated meant "having" Latin, and later on, it meant having French, and today mostly English [...] Learning these languages as codes is a mark of privilege.' She continues:

The dominant classes wrote the books used in their schools to reflect their privileged linguistic and cultural practices, their racial images, their funds of knowledge. For these dominant classes, learning to read and write in school meant to bring themselves into being as advantaged groups, developing subjectivities of power and privilege.

While García generalizes the complex social functions of classics throughout the centuries (see below), I am interested in her description of 'having' Latin, or indeed ancient Greek or classics, as a tool to bring privilege into being: she argues that having access to this knowledge reinforces access to other societally valuable resources. The verb 'having' implies that access is more important than content, and that what 'classics', 'Latin', and 'ancient Greek' entail is rather more subjective than you might think: is it grammar (and if so: which grammar)? Is it texts (and which texts do we include, from which period/s)? Is it culture (and are there [sub]-cultures we don't study)? And when can you say that you 'know' ('have') Latin or ancient Greek?[37] Should you be able to read Tacitus or Thucydides at sight? The interpretation of these terms is in effect not stable, even if the exclusionary symbolic value is. Although we can talk about 'ancient Greek', 'Latin', or indeed 'classics', these terms are actually 'symbols that have been taken from their contexts and now float as free radicals' to which everyone is able to attribute their definition of choice to use for their own agenda.[38]

This does mean that *anyone* may appropriate antiquity for their own purposes. Just as elite social groups create a code of belonging, marginalized social groups have also found access to classics in the past centuries – which nuances García's argument – whether to rise through (or rebel against) the social ranks, access beauty associated with high culture, and/or fight for emancipation. In this way, subaltern social groups such as working-class groups, feminist or queer activists, and colonized social groups have long appropriated the study of antiquity and redefined what they consider classical 'knowledge', so it becomes 'a site of cultural resistance', sometimes in a formal setting but often outside the classroom.[39] Of course, even if this appropriation of classics has been instrumental in defining their distinct identity, it is important to acknowledge that their response to the ancient world was based at least partly on its existing function as social code classics played for the elite. Yet it is possible to speak of a 'democratic turn' in classics,[40] whereby access to its knowledge – whatever that entails specifically – is being increased through popular culture and, indeed, education, as I will presently discuss.

1.3.2 Classics and educational barriers

In general, classics education can still be considered exclusionary. We need not look to the past to consider this: if we merely consider the examples of contemporary Flanders and the UK, the issue fast becomes apparent. Latin remains a strong subject in the Flemish secondary school system: even considering dwindling uptake, most secondary schools retain a Latin curriculum, at least for cognitively strong pupils of what is called the 'A-stream' (an educational trajectory which stands in contrast with the more practical education of the 'B-stream', where no classics is taught). According to the latest figures, 9% of all secondary school pupils studied Latin in 2020–21.[41] Ancient Greek is a wholly different matter: it may only be started during pupils' first year of Latin, and is thus solely accessible to those pupils who have already started studying Latin. Because of those restrictions, in 2020–21 only 1% of all secondary school pupils studied it. In theory, any pupil moving from primary to secondary school is allowed to opt for Latin as their educational trajectory as long as they have achieved their primary school certification. However, in reality, pupils from the most affluent socioeconomic backgrounds are almost twice as likely to choose Latin as their peers from the lowest socioeconomic context.[42] This figure reveals that barriers exist which discourage pupils from deprived socioeconomic backgrounds from partaking in Latin, and hence also Greek. These barriers exist, to return to Nicaise (2000), on both the 'demand' and 'supply' side. Alongside the educational structures biased against pupils from a lower socioeconomic background and ethnic minority, unconscious bias among teachers ('supply') is one such barrier: research demonstrates, for example, that teachers are less likely to encourage pupils from an ethnic minority background (who are more likely to grow up in a low socioeconomic context) to take up Latin at secondary level than their peers, even when they demonstrate comparable aptitude.[43] This is of course a generalization, as many teachers work hard to counter inequity; however, we are all affected by unconscious bias as we are unaware of it, and it is important that we do not shy away from this admission, painful though it is. Another factor is unconscious bias on the part of pupils and their parents ('demand'), whether they reject Latin voluntarily because their parents did not study it or because 'it's not for them'.[44] As the head teacher of one primary school I currently work with summarized unambiguously:

> We notice that explicit and implicit prejudice from society, family, friends, and sometimes teachers, as well as the home situation (such as deprivation or another cultural background), mean that our pupils do not always get all the opportunities they deserve. In the transition from primary to secondary education, the step towards studying Latin (and then Greek) is hardly ever taken. After all, it is assumed that this is not an option for them.

The head teacher's reflection correlates with the data: there exists an incongruity between a meritocratic education system in theory and a hierarchical and indeed inequitable system in practice, with classics acting as one particular signifier to differentiate people's social status.

In the UK, educational structures and barriers may be expressed differently, but access to Latin and Greek subjects at secondary school level is equally problematic. As Steven Hunt and Arlene Holmes-Henderson demonstrate (2021: 2), 'Latin is very much the preserve of independent schools and state-maintained selective schools in the South and South-East of England. Greek is almost completely absent from the state-maintained sector.' Non-linguistic subjects (which as of yet do not exist in Flanders) such as Classical Civilization and Ancient History do have a moderate appeal among pupils, at least more than the ancient languages, but the situation is dire. Hunt and Holmes-Henderson (2021:18) conclude that 'access to classics in schools relies on wealth or luck' and describe this inequality of access to the study of the ancient world as 'classics poverty'.

Other countries have their own unique education systems and therefore the precise shape and function of classics as gatekeeper can differ, yet the exclusionary system is real there too. In the Netherlands, for example, pupils attending the top educational tier at secondary school, the Gymnasium, study Latin and/or Greek alongside other theoretical subjects, with a particular aim to prepare them for university studies, while pupils attending any of the other tiers have little or no access to classics.[45] In France, educational reform in 2018 led to a fast reduction of Latin pupil numbers, since the subject area 'literature, languages and cultures of antiquity' is only offered in a small selection of schools.[46] In Germany, classics is predominantly studied at the Gymnasium, yet pupils with an ethnic minority background are vastly underrepresented there in comparison with the other types of secondary school.[47] I lack the space to explore every country,[48] but these examples reveal that access to classical subjects in education occurs along similar lines as access to privileged education based on intersections – unique to each country and region – of class, ethnicity, region, and culture. While Bulwer (2018: 69), a keen observer of classics education in Europe, notes: 'it is now generally accepted in all countries that Latin and Classics should be offered to all pupils irrespective of background', 'should' is the key word in his observation, as the reality unfortunately tells a different story. Access to classics implies access to lower pupil–teacher ratios and more extensive school resources, with a higher likelihood of higher grades and access to (top) universities and better employment. This is confirmed by research from Belgium, which reveals that university students who have studied Latin or Greek alongside advanced maths or science subjects, on average, have a 38% higher chance of getting a university degree than students who studied any other subjects at secondary school; there is, moreover, overlap with students who have the Belgian nationality and are not from an inner-city background.[49] Research from Germany reveals the tangible effects of studying Latin on opportunities in later life: people who studied Latin are considered higher in status than those who studied French, and are, in another study more likely to be invited for job interviews.[50] 'Classics poverty' in education, in short, can and should not be considered separately from the issues I discussed in the previous section, namely educational inequity and indeed multidimensional child poverty.

The problem with an exclusionary formal education system is, to state the obvious, that not many people have access to certain subjects. In many countries over the past century, classical subjects have struggled to recruit pupils in competition with more immediately practical subjects. A long and arduous road has since begun to try and reclaim a key place for Latin and Greek in the secondary school curriculum, which forms part of the 'democratic turn' I discussed above, and is generally achieved in the form of 'widening participation' of classics either within or outside the educational curriculum,[51] to what are considered non-traditional target groups among children. The arguments are often essentialist, identity-based, or utilitarian in nature. Essentialist arguments suggest there is universal value to be found in ancient Greek and Roman antiquity, which makes these subjects worth studying (perhaps more than others), while identity-based arguments propose a common heritage to which much of Europe, the US, and the Mediterranean can look for its roots. The utilitarian arguments, finally, are based on the notion that learning Latin or ancient Greek has a positive effect on pupils' native language/s, on subsequent learning of modern languages, and a far transfer effect on logical or mathematical skills.[52] These arguments are as old as our education systems, and while they are often cited and there is indeed much anecdotal evidence from learners, the actual research findings are not as clear as one might expect. While there has been strong evidence in the past century to propose a positive effect on native languages such as English and German, impact on modern languages and far transfer is less attested.[53]

However, whichever arguments proponents of the study of classics use to support it, widening participation is inevitably ideologically tinted and indeed aimed at rendering authority to the selected ideology. I am not arguing that this is necessarily wrong and I am certainly not arguing that classics does not deserve support – this book aims to offer a strong case in support of classics in primary schools which may also have a positive knock-on effect on classics at secondary and university level – but it is important to be aware of the underlying ideological mechanics which drive us and others. In mainland Europe, for example, a recent call to action to bring Latin and ancient Greek to more secondary school pupils has been made by French education minister Jean-Michel Blanquer, in a joint statement with his colleagues from Greece, Italy, and Cyprus. The joint declaration speaks of Latin and ancient Greek as 'the living and structuring heritage of a common branch of European and Mediterranean culture', and argues that

> learning the languages and cultures of antiquity, the practice of translation, and the understanding of a humanist culture allow for the development of fundamental knowledge and tools for reflection, necessary for [...] the emancipation of pupils, for European citizenship, and the defence of common values.[54]

The identity-based definition of classics reinforcing European identity is bolstered by utilitarian elements. However, in an interview, Blanquer, asked why he is such a staunch proponent of classical languages, not only talked about wanting to broaden access to Latin and Greek beyond the elite, but also revealed that his campaign is in fact part of his war on 'woke-ness', which he fears is drifting from across the channel and the Atlantic to 'cancel' the classics and what he considers 'traditional' culture.[55] Whatever you may think of woke-ness, Blanquer's ideological agenda in bringing classics to the masses now becomes clear: by teaching them Latin or Greek, he wants to involve young people in his vision of a traditional France and Europe. Yet the extent to which his support for classics is genuine must be questioned. Blanquer indeed made similar noises concerning the support needed for classics in 2018,[56] yet did very little to support actual classics teachers and pupils. In fact, the primary reason for the recent stark decline of classics teaching in France is argued to be his own curriculum reform.[57] His current plans to offer Latin and Greek to pupils studying technical subjects was therefore received with reservations by French teachers, who questioned the plan's feasibility in the light of the current classics teacher shortage.[58]

Widening participation in classics as proposed by policymakers can therefore not necessarily be taken at face value, based on the ethereal beauty of classical literature, but must be contextualized in the development of specific political agendas. Much as I love classics, I become guarded when politicians propound their definition of 'classics' – invariably dreaming of idealized rational thinkers and models of traditional/democratic/Western virtue which the Greeks and Romans as a whole certainly never were – to further their ideological campaigns. This jars painfully with the lived experiences of both teachers and pupils, who need logistical and financial support rather than political grandstanding, and the latter of whom take years before they even get to read those texts so beloved by politicians.

One of the pillars of social justice is the removal of social barriers, and one might therefore reasonably argue that widening participation in classics is a clear step towards educational equity. However, *merely* widening participation in classics – as Blanquer, for example, proposes – does not necessarily lead to social justice for pupils. In order for pupils from hitherto excluded social groups to gain meaningful access to the subject area, they need to be given a voice. To this end, it is necessary not merely to provide them with access to existing educational structures, but to adapt those structures so all pupils can contribute to knowledge creation from their own background, by using the teaching of classics as a transformative tool. Widening participation needs to be married to changes to pedagogy in order to activate the potential of classics as a tool for social justice. There are many inspiring projects worldwide which aim at increasing access to classics, but two examples of teacher-led educational reforms at secondary school level demonstrate how widening participation and didactic inclusivity go hand in hand when working towards social justice at an educational level.[59]

In Germany, where Latin still has a strong position in the secondary curriculum,[60] educational innovation was driven not from an urge to 'save' classics, but rather from a drive to work towards cultural integration. The innovative *Pons Latinus* ('The Latin Bridge') project has indeed reframed Latin learning as a tool to help children from a – predominantly Turkish – minority background learn German.[61] Latin is reframed as a linguistic bridge between Turkish or other first languages (L1) and German second language (L2). Widening participation in classics among migration-background pupils is thus complemented by an adapted didactic methodology, focused on providing a linguistic bridge between L1 and L2.

A similar approach can be perceived in another exciting practice, this time from Switzerland. After a government-led curriculum overhaul to broaden the *Gesamtschulen* (middle school, the first two years of secondary school) so all pupils would study together before they are separated in high school, it turned out no provision had been made to include Latin at middle school. Teaching practitioners thus worked together to design the course book *Aurea Bulla* with cognitively diverse pupil groups from the *Gesamtschulen* in mind,[62] and tested its impact in 2017–19. The didactic approach focuses on strengthening pupils' 'intuitive and metacognitive linguistic competences'. Katharina Wesselmann, currently professor in classics teacher training at Kiel, observed that the 'connection between economic status and the performance [i.e. overall literacy, in German and other modern languages of pupils taking part in the course] decreased [significantly] over the two years of the course'.[63]

The language ideology underpinning both projects is very different from Blanquer's, as it is focused on bringing pupils' backgrounds into the Latin classroom rather than bringing a fixed notion of Latin out to them, and embeds widening participation in an adapted pedagogy.

This discussion has demonstrated that widening access to classics among non-traditional social groups of pupils is never ideologically neutral, but rather intrinsically based on political and language ideology. Whether a reactionary return to traditional subjects and values, or a social justice-based campaign to bolster equity in an inclusive society, however, the common theme is that classics – in whatever form – is endowed with a symbolic place in our heritage and thereby has the power to lend authority to those who study it. Needless to say, unless drastic educational reform is enacted, the educational inequity which accompanies the widening gulf between children growing up in privilege and those growing up in poverty will remain in place. However, it is precise because classics traditionally acted as gatekeeper that it has a key role to play as a potential gateway, not merely at secondary school but also in primary education, as I will demonstrate in the next chapter.

1.4 Conclusion and reflection tools

This chapter was by far the most theoretical in the book, and we will get to the practical shortly. It was, however, necessary to frame my social justice approach in the global issues of social inequity and multidimensional poverty, their effect on and materialization in education, and the place of classics in these mechanics. For it is vital, before we start our practical discussion, to be aware of the ideological underpinnings and implications of offering classics to non-traditional target groups. I have argued that it is not sufficient to merely 'widen access' to classics among underrepresented groups by bringing classics *out to* them. That would merely bring them into the existing system, thus further strengthening the status quo rather than enacting change. In order to provide traditionally excluded groups with a way *into* the field of classics, they need to be given a voice, which requires a redefinition of 'classics'. In Chapter 2, I will therefore start exploring how widening participation in classics has the potential for increasing educational equity at primary school level. Chapters 3 and 4 then explore the practical didactic approach I take in teaching classics at primary school by reframing what 'classics' means. Chapter 3 outlines six steps one might take in order to make classics accessible in an inclusive classroom, with the potential of enabling 'transformative learning' among pupils. In Chapter 4, I discuss course outlines, particular lesson plans, and activities in the *Ancient Greeks – Young Heroes* project to make the case for the practical application of the concept of 'translanguaging' – a current Modern Foreign Language approach which moves away from strict L1-to-L2 learning to focus on developing pupils' entire linguistic repertoire – to the teaching of ancient Greek and Latin. These three chapters outline how widening participation and an adapted pedagogy go hand in hand when using classics as a tool to work towards social justice. There is, however, a third factor which I have not yet mentioned, and that is community engagement. It is indeed vital that pupils' classroom classics learning is embedded into their social background in order to enable meaningful transformative learning. Chapter 5 therefore reflects on the importance of community engagement with the various stakeholders of primary school classics: learners and teachers, families and communities, the media and policy makers. Each of these four activities – widening participation, transformative learning, a translanguaging approach, and community engagement – by themselves can make a valuable contribution to improving social and educational equity. Yet it is a strong focus on, and combination of, all four actions which I will argue can work towards social justice, by enabling traditionally marginalized groups to take part in the knowledge creation narrative of classics as we move further into the twenty-first century.

This book aims to be a toolkit, and this chapter has offered a long and theoretical – necessarily generalizing – introduction. So that readers may use the book actively, each chapter ends with a series of reflection tools. The answer categories have the following key:

− −   This is definitely not a priority for me.
−   Ipay attention to this from time to time.
− +   I would like to pay more attention to this, but I'm not sure how.
+   Iregularly pay attention to this.
+ +   This is an integral part of my current thinking.

I would therefore now invite you to reflect on your current practice based on the discussion in this introductory chapter (Table 1.1).

For some readers, these tools will be new, for others well-trodden ground. Some will be encouraged by my discussion, others will reject it; some are interested in the big picture, others in the details. My purpose in inviting you to consider these statements at the end of each chapter is to invite you to reflect on your current – and potentially, future – practice and thinking.

Table 1.1 Reflection tools

	− −	−	− +	+	+ +
It is clear to me which children in my country or area are disproportionately at risk of growing up in multidimensional poverty.					
I am aware of the inequity and hierarchies present in the educational system in my country or area.					
I reflect on the social functions of 'classics' in my country or area, within the context of language ideologies.					
I'm aware of the current status of Latin, Greek, and other classics-related subjects, in my local education system, and which (in)visible barriers restrict access.					

Notes

1 See www.literacythroughclassics.weebly.com.
2 I will retain the term 'classics' (without capital letter) to refer to the linguistic study of ancient Greek and Roman antiquity. I am fully aware of the difficulties inherent in the term (Quinn 2017), but in order to refer to the academic and educational field rather than the content, I retain it as recognizable shorthand.
3 See www.ancientgreeksyoungheroes.ugent.be.
4 Härkönen 2018, Crabtree & Kluch 2020.
5 Belgium has a federal government, but education is in the hands of the three political 'regions': the Flemish (Dutch-speaking), Brussels, and Walloon (French-speaking) regions. My project focuses on the Flemish region, since Ghent University is situated there. For this reason, I will speak about Flanders or the Flemish region in this book, and not Belgium, from an educational point.
6 UNDP & Oxford Poverty and Human Development Initiative 2020: 4–5. For a discussion of how (multidimensional) poverty is measured, see Beck et al. 2020.
7 Definition by the Flemish Government's child support organization *Opgroeien* ('Growing Up'); my translation of the Dutch-medium definition at www.opgroeien.be/cijfers-en-publicaties/kansarmoede.
8 https://www.unicef.org/social-policy/child-poverty.
9 These are the figures from 2020, derived from the website *Opgroeien* (see n. 8): https://www.opgroeien.be/cijfers-en-publicaties/kansarmoede/ vlaams-gewest-en-provincie and Beke 2020: 10–12.
10 These are the figures from 2020, see Welsh Government 2021.
11 See www.unicef.org/social-policy/child-poverty.
12 Mood & Jonsson 2016, Kalthoff 2018.
13 UNICEF 2021.
14 See p. 4.
15 Valcke & Decraene 2020, 4th edition: 97.
16 van den Bergh et al. 2010, Vantieghem 2016: 72–73. See Hattie 2009: 31–36 on the effect of pupils', parental, and teachers' expectations on pupils' results.
17 Franck & Nicaise (2019: 3): 'social background, educational segregation, and cognitive achievement arguably impact on each other in an escalating movement, so they start working cumulatively throughout a child's school career' (my translation of the Dutch). See Nicaise et al. 2000 for a European study, Reay 2017 for British findings.
18 See https://www.isc.co.uk/.
19 Valcke & Standaert 2020, 2nd edition: 121, Goossens et al. 2015, Vanderstichele 2020.
20 Benson et al. 2015: 39. Also Butler & Hamnett 2007.
21 UK: Vidal Rodeiro & Zanini 2015 though Ndaji et al. 2016: 43 argue that independent school pupils outperform their peers. Flanders: Vanwynsberghe 2017 and Frank & Nicaise 2019.
22 For the UK, Green & Kynaston 2019; for Flanders, Goossens et al. 2015: 4, and Franck & Nicaise 2019: 53.

23 See n. 21.
24 Henderson et al. 2020, Sutton Trust 2019.
25 PISA UGent 2018: 48–49.
26 Vantieghem 2016.
27 Hattie 2009: 63.
28 TIMSS & PIRLS International Study Center 2016.
29 Valcke & Standaert 2020, 2nd edition: 108–14, Ross 2021: 8–9.
30 DESA 2006: 6–7.
31 Ross 2021: 11.
32 Freire 1970, Bourdieu 1986.
33 Edgar Allen Poe 1831, *To Helen.*
34 Stray 2021. See also Gerhards et al. 2019: 314–15.
35 Woolard 2020: 1.
36 Woolard 2020: 2.
37 Hall's 2021 study on the emergence of the term 'classics' sheds light on the negotiations surrounding the meaning of the term.
38 Hardwick 2013: 28.
39 E.g. Greenwood 2010, Vasunia 2013, Wyles & Hall 2016, Richardson 2018, Hall & Stead 2020.
40 Hardwick 2013.
41 See http://www.classicavlaanderen.be/informatie/cijfermateriaal/index.html.
42 Boone 2011: 22, specifically 57% versus 29%, and Van Praag et al. 2019: 177.
43 Goosen et al. 2017: 113–14.
44 Boone 2011: 23.
45 Merry & Boterman 2020, Bigiman 2022.
46 Bonod 2021.
47 Kuhlmann 2020: 2.
48 European Commission/EACEA/Eurydice 2017: 51–53 for data regarding all EU countries. See Bulwer 2006 and 2018 (Europe), Bostick 2021 (US), Sawert 2018 (Germany).
49 Rombaut et al. 2006: 6.
50 Gerhards et al. 2019; Sawert 2016.
51 E.g. Holmes-Henderson, Hunt, Musié 2018, Holmes-Henderson 2023.
52 Gerhards et al. 2019.
53 For an overview of studies about English, see Bracke & Bradshaw 2021, and also Holmes-Henderson 2023; for an overview of German studies, see Gerhards et al. 2019, and recently Goik 2021.
54 Blanquer et al. 2021 (my translation of the French). See also Ko 2000, chapter 2.
55 Ono-dit-Biot 2021.
56 Heidsieck 2018.
57 Bonod 2021.
58 Erner 2021.
59 For an example from the US, where Latin is being taught in a secondary school with a majority of Latinx pupils, averaging 'two years or more behind grade level with serious math and literacy deficits, poor study habits, negative attitudes toward school, and low language skills', see Janoff 2014: 259.

60 Gerhards et al. 2019.
61 Kipf 2014; Grosse 2017; Freund & Janssen 2017; Kipf 2019.
62 See also the course book *Suburani* in the UK; Delaney et al. 2021.
63 Pandey 2021 and Wesselmann 2021.

2 Raising young heroes – teaching Latin and ancient Greek at primary school

2.1 Classics at primary school in the US and Europe

The previous chapter explored how widening participation in classics at the secondary school level can be applied to improve educational equity. In practice, however, it can be difficult for secondary school boards to offer classics within their curriculum, even if they are persuaded by the potential benefits for pupils. The hierarchical education systems of many countries indeed preclude access to classics for many pupils not on the correct pathway, as teachers are under pressure to deliver learning objectives for each subject in a tightly packed curriculum. In most countries, the primary school curriculum, by contrast, has a little more breathing room, and classics can fit in with curriculums on literacy, 'foreign' languages, history, or citizenship, to name but a few options. Since, as the previous chapter outlined, educational inequity starts much earlier than secondary school, intervening at an earlier age by widening participation in classics at primary school level therefore makes sense not only from a logistical point of view but also from a social justice perspective. In the US and throughout Europe, teaching classics at primary school is indeed already being done, often with tremendous success. Therefore, let us first explore what groundbreaking work has already been done by projects to move the benchmark of what classics can entail.

2.1.1 'Latin words are like sticks of dynamite':[1] Latin in US primary schools

Since the 1960s at least, classics – particularly Latin – has been offered to pupils at primary school, and this for various ideological reasons, not necessarily with the aim of increasing social justice. Interestingly, it was in the US of the 1960s and 1970s – where Latin was (and remains)

DOI: 10.4324/9781003229742-2

accessible chiefly to select secondary-school pupils[2] – that social justice–driven Latin projects first started popping up at primary or 'elementary' school, specifically for 'under-privileged inner-city children'.[3] The key reason was an increasing worry among educators about a veritable literacy crisis taking hold of the younger generation in the US[4] that was not only class- but also ethnicity-driven.[5] Since traditional programmes to improve literacy levels did not always have the desired effect, the initiative was taken to offer Latin to these social groups, since it was generally held that learning Latin, with so many English derivatives and applications in technical jargon, would be beneficial. The aim of these programmes was rooted in a social justice language ideology, ensuring 'that all children – average, slow, and gifted – can profit from some type of experience with Latin. [These projects] squarely reject the traditional view that foreign languages are for college-bound [pupils] only'. The courses offered a specifically 'humanistic experience' in order to increase pupils' English skills as well as their 'awareness […] of the diversities within a society and an understanding and appreciation of these diversities'.[6] To include children from all abilities and backgrounds, particularly in the inner-city contexts of Philadelphia and Washington DC (which Nancy Mavrogenes called as close to an 'all-ghetto school system' as one might get in the US),[7] 'the exercises [were made] easier with constant repetition and reinforcement and many translation aids. Material [was] incorporated from African authors (Terence, Apuleius, St. Augustine) and on slavery and minority groups in the Roman empire'.[8]

This example clearly demonstrates the point with which I ended the previous chapter, namely that widening participation needs to be combined with didactic adaptations in order to be successful. The results of these projects, reported by Rudolph Masciantonio 1975, Mavrogenes 1977, and Lewis Sussman 1978, were indeed astonishing: in comparison with control groups, pupils consistently 'climbed from the lowest level of reading ability to the highest level for their grade' and outperformed their peers in control groups.[9] If the instructions from the School District of Philadelphia's teachers' guide for *How the Romans lived and spoke* are anything to go by, I can easily believe children were enchanted! In lesson 2, for example, in order to explain why pupils should learn Latin, the teachers' guide suggests the teacher asks …

… how many children have ever heard of BLACK POWER. Ask the same question about WHITE POWER and FLOWER POWER. Tell them that Latin gives them a power which is greater in many ways than all three put together, viz. WORD POWER.

Say WORD POWER in a loud voice and have the children repeat it. Tell them that Latin words are like sticks of dynamite. Every time you learn one Latin word it explodes into many English words. Breaking up some chalk into small pieces and letting the chalk scatter when you say the work "explodes" is an effective dramatic device at this point.[10]

The focus on drama and engagement with pupils' particular lived experience must have been exciting. For pupils growing up in deprived circumstances, engaging with this 'multisensory' approach, in which they also practised listening and speaking before reading and writing, was clearly a joyful experience. However, alongside the actual (adapted) pedagogy, the creators of this project acknowledged the importance of educational 'access'. Listed among the general objectives of the School District of Philadelphia's course was the aim 'to improve the child's self-image by giving him the *opportunity* to study a subject area *with which he might not otherwise identify*' (my italics).[11] Research suggests that learning Latin may have a bigger cognitive impact on pupils from deprived socioeconomic backgrounds than on their more affluent peers,[12] which corroborates the importance of being granted access to such a highly valued subject, though the teaching method and content are equally significant, as the next chapters will discuss.

There were a number of similar projects in the US between the 1960s and 1980s, predominantly situated on the Northeast coast and in California,[13] most of which reported a positive impact of Latin lessons on pupils' literacy in English and on their educational aspirations.[14] Indeed, some of them also focused on Spanish literacy, such as the Language Transfer Project, started in 1972 by Albert Baca, which taught Latin roots and affixes specifically to 10- to 12-year old native Spanish speakers as 'a bridge from Spanish to English'.[15] While those projects no longer exist, since 2013 the Aequora project integrates Masciantonio's method into a social justice approach based on modern literacy models, in order to teach Latin to public school and at-risk children in the US with the help of university student volunteers. Aequora's aim is to reinforce English and Spanish literacy while also 'prompting [pupils] to think about the relationships among colonization, culture, and language through the story of children in Roman Spain'.[16] The Youth Classics Institute Ascanius similarly aims to 'encourage today's youth to think critically about ancient societies and compare them to their daily life in the modern world', by offering grants which support students and teachers to offer classics at primary school.[17] While these are explicit social justice–driven projects, Latin also persists in private primary schools throughout the US, though I am told no precise figures exist on the number of pupils that study it.

2.1.2   From the UK to Greece: primary school classics projects in Europe

More recently, classics teaching as a means of raising literacy and aspirations among primary school pupils also took off in the UK, particularly thanks to the financial support offered by the charity Classics for All.[18] The initial impetus was Barbara Bell's Latin course *Minimus*, which narrates the story of a mouse living with a human family at the Roman site of Vindolanda by Hadrian's Wall. First published in 1999 and rapidly expanded to include a huge range of accessible teaching resources, this engaging course book has enabled countless children worldwide to come into contact with Latin and Roman culture ever since and continues to be popular.[19] In the early 2000s, two more Latin widening participation projects were initiated. In 2006, the Iris Project started up with the express aim of offering Latin 'to large mixed-ability classes in inner city schools' with the help of student volunteers, and in 2007 the Latin Programme started supporting pupils' English literacy skills in the London area, primarily by teaching grammar directly and often kinaesthetically.[20] I first came into contact with The Iris Project in 2010, when this project was already working with the University of Oxford and King's College London to provide Latin classes for disenfranchised children in local areas. On the basis of my communication with Lorna Robinson, coordinator of the Iris Project, I decided to start up a project at Swansea. I designed the *Literacy through Classics* project, through which my students taught Latin and classical culture at primary school.[21] From setting up and coordinating this project, I gained the experience which I then applied in the Flemish *Young Heroes* project I will introduce below.

In 2014, Latin and ancient Greek became optional languages in the English primary school curriculum alongside modern languages, and in 2019 Wales followed when it reframed 'modern foreign languages' as 'international languages' which included Latin and ancient Greek.[22] This integration into the primary school curriculum is unique in Europe as far as I can tell, and currently, up to 4% of primary schools in England reportedly teach Latin – I was as yet unable to access figures for Wales. To support primary schools wishing to incorporate Latin or ancient Greek, there has been a proliferation of course books: Classics for All offers the *Maximum Classics* course, which combines Latin learning with a focus on literacy and culture; *Mega Greek* and

Basil Batrakhos, which offer literacy-based introductory courses to ancient Greek; and a *Word Roots* course, which combines roots from Latin and ancient Greek to improve literacy directly.[23] Lorna Robinson's text-based course books *Telling Tales in Latin* and *Telling Tales in Greek* teach Latin and Greek through mythological stories.[24] The free online *Primary Latin course* by the Hands Up Education charity, based on archaeological evidence and incorporating photos of Herculaneum, takes a nuanced, inclusive approach of antiquity and has great accessibility.[25] As you can see, there is a wealth of projects and resources in the UK for teachers wanting to get started with classics at primary school. There is as yet limited research on the impact of these courses,[26] but Classics for All states that '90% of pupils surveyed [...] reported that learning classics had a positive impact on their attainment, cultural awareness and aspirations and a growing number of pupils supported by us are now studying classics at examination level or at university'.[27]

It was only when I moved back to Belgium that I became aware of primary school classics projects in other countries. In France, the *Nausicaa* project, located in Marseilles and driven by a group of secondary school teacher volunteers, has been teaching ancient Greek through fables and myths to children as young as four since 1997.[28] Their focus on inclusive teaching means the project has had some remarkable successes with pupils struggling with learning difficulties. Interestingly, *Nausicaa* lessons are integrated into each school's curriculum, which renders schools' engagement with the project sustainable. In one school in the Netherlands, final-year secondary school pupils are teaching introductory Latin to primary school children. In Greece, the *Elliniki Agogi* organization offers (paid) lessons of ancient Greek for primary school-age children.[29] These projects, which were discussed at an international conference I co-organized with Steven Hunt (Cambridge) and Lidewij van Gils (Amsterdam) in January 2022, aim at widening participation (they increase the number of pupils studying classics), though not all of them are necessarily social justice–driven. Their target demographic at primary school may be in the same socioeconomic bracket as those pupils who study Latin and Greek at secondary school.

In short, there is a strong tradition of teaching particularly Latin at primary school in the US and increasingly in the UK, while more isolated projects exist in Europe. Every one of these projects works towards specific aims driven by language ideology, whether to bolster the number of pupils studying classics at secondary school or increase literacy and aspirations among non-traditional target groups. These goals are not mutually exclusive, and they may indeed go together (more about this in the next chapters). My own project positions itself deliberately within a social justice narrative, shaped by the child poverty debate in Flanders. It follows particularly in the footsteps of the US projects and some of the recent work done in the UK, intentionally setting out to break down barriers and disrupt damaging narratives regarding the abilities of pupils from disadvantaged social groups.

2.2 Introducing the *Ancient Greeks – Young Heroes* project

When I set up the *Literacy through Classics* project at Swansea University in 2011, I had a double objective in mind. First, I wanted to introduce pupils from this (former) mining region to a subject to which they did not traditionally have access. In this widening participation aim, I followed in the footsteps of many projects before me. My second aim was to offer my university students teaching experience that would give them the opportunity to be admitted to classics teacher training degree schemes, similar to other universities which had already partnered with The Iris Project. To this end, my students received teacher training to offer Latin and ancient history to primary school pupils. There were usually ten hours of lessons per semester, taught by groups of two to five students, who could participate either as part of their degree or on a voluntary basis. The project grew each year and became a success in the South Wales area. My focus was primarily on raising pupils' academic aspirations, so I was pleasantly surprised when I received feedback from school teachers that their literacy levels increased after (and because of?) their participation in my project. It also became clear to me that pupils' contact with the university students was as important as the actual language learning, since university students acted as role models for pupils whose families had not had access to university.[30] It is based on this expertise that I started the *Ancient Greeks – Young Heroes* project once I began working at Ghent University.

2.2.1 From literacy to young heroes: redefining ancient Greek

In Flanders, child poverty levels continue to increase, but certain social groups – such as children from an ethnic minority background, from single-mother families, and those raised in an urban setting – are disproportionately affected.[31] Access to ancient Greek is intrinsically restricted among this disadvantaged group, as secondary school pupils in Flanders must have studied Latin before they are allowed to take up ancient Greek.[32] Since pupils with an ethnic minority background are encouraged to take up Latin disproportionally less often than their peers at secondary school (even when their cognitive abilities are the same), their access to the study of ancient Greek is virtually non-existent. In order to challenge this educational inequity and help disrupt the downward motivational spiral affecting the most vulnerable children in society, I designed the *Ancient Greeks – Young Heroes* project at Ghent University. Through this project, teacher trainee students teach ancient Greek in Flemish primary school with high numbers of pupils growing up in multidimensional poverty. I consciously chose a name not connected to literacy, unlike my project in the UK, but which expresses the support I want to give children growing up in difficult circumstances by means of ancient Greek study. More than literacy skills, the *Young Heroes* project as it has become known, seeks to raise pupils' self-esteem and academic aspirations, by demonstrating to both pupils and teachers that these children are capable of more. I also realized that, while Latin may have been more meaningful in the Welsh context (Greek is not well known while Latin is associated with the privilege of private schools), ancient Greek revealed itself to be more meaningful in the Flemish context, because of its more exclusive status.

As I have a limited number of teacher trainee students each year, we work with two local primary schools. Since 2019, around 20 students have taught 200 pupils. Each year, pupils ages 10–12, in the final two years of primary school, receive 10–12 hours of ancient Greek over a period of five weeks. The majority of these pupils do not speak Dutch at home which tends to cause issues in their schooling (see below); many of them have learning difficulties. Lessons are taught by Ghent University students who are training to be secondary school teachers of ancient Greek. As at Swansea University, they receive teacher training regarding the specific pedagogy from me, as well as extensive weekly guidance. They can either take part as a volunteer or through a module, for which they are assessed on the basis of lesson plans, a lesson observation, and a self-reflective report. The way pupils are taught ancient Greek is not traditional. As I will explore in Chapter 3, a self-reflective approach is applied throughout in order to facilitate transformative learning. Moreover, the ancient Greek language particularly is taught in a non-linear and culturally sensitive way – more on this in Chapter 4. This approach was chosen because, in the Flemish region, full access to education among certain ethnic minority groups – which form a significant social group at risk of living in poverty – is particularly hindered by the language debate. Because most people moving to Flanders do not know Dutch, learning Dutch is considered key to 'complete' integration. There is, however, an – often invisible and ideologically based – dichotomy between 'prestige' home languages such as English or French, which are considered to have a high socioeconomic value, and 'plebeian' home languages such as Arabic, Turkish, or Russian, which are widely believed to hinder integration.[33] In Flanders there exists an unremitting political discourse concerning the use of pupils' home languages at school, ignoring research findings on the benefits of any multilingualism for children.[34] Pupils with 'plebeian' home languages tend to have their multilingualism disregarded and struggle with academic self-confidence more than their peers. The *Young Heroes* project promotes inclusivity by integrating pupils' home languages in ancient Greek lessons. By giving all home languages an equal function in the lessons and by celebrating multilingualism and intercultural learning (see Chapter 4), the project aims to support educational and social equity.

The specific pedagogy and inclusive approach to ancient Greek will be explored in greater detail in the following chapters. However, this introduction to the project reveals that, while classics might have a role to play in any primary school curriculum, it is important to consider not only the educational context in your area but also the political context in which you're working, in addition to your pupils' needs within that system. As we have already discussed, it is not possible to teach classics in an ideological vacuum.

2.2.2 *'It was fun and I miss the teachers': the project's impact*

Pupil feedback on the project is incredibly positive (see Figure 2.1).[35] In anonymous end-of-project questionnaires, pupils are invited to circle a happy emoji, a neutral emoji, or a negative emoji when answering questions on how they felt about the project as a whole, learning new words, talking about culture and myths, playing games, and engaging with the students. The vast majority of pupils circle the happy emoji, and it is not unusual for pupils to add exclamation marks or 'super happy' emojis.[36] On open questions, children consistently comment positively on the cognitive challenge which the lessons provide. Asked which lesson they liked the most, 'All of it' is a common answer![37] One pupil commented '[A]ll of them, but I liked the last one with the food and making the text. And the second [lesson] I [also] liked because I found the gods interesting. And I really liked the play! Well done.' Another pupil said: 'The Minotaur because I thought he was funny', and added, 'PS I think the lessons are super nice and I'm sorry they're finished, I'll miss it, you taught very nice lessons.' These are typical comments. Other pupils say they particularly liked 'taking part in plays', 'already knowing something', the Greek 'alphabet song', or 'the Greek gods'.

Interestingly, percentages of positive evaluation by pupils studying ancient Greek in Flanders correspond closely to the evaluation by primary school pupils who studied Latin during my time coordinating the Literacy through Classics project in Swansea (see Figure 2.2).[38] Each year, pupil satisfaction with all aspects of the project (language, games, culture, engagement with student-teachers, and the overall project) is extremely high, and this has been a stable factor over the years I have worked with children from deprived backgrounds in primary schools. Figures 2.1 and 2.2 both reveal that enjoyment of the linguistic element is slightly less high than the other elements, but this in fact means that the project is about more than just the language: it is about engagement with language and intercultural reflection in a playful way, through communication with the student-teachers. The positive pupil evaluations highlight that the pedagogical approach my students and I apply is successful in reaching its target group. The head teacher of one of our project schools confirms the project's impact:

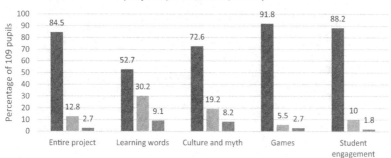

Figure 2.1 Pupil enjoyment of the *Ancient Greeks – Young Heroes* project (2019, 2021, 2022).

The great thing about the *Ancient Greeks – Young Heroes* project is that nobody has any prior knowledge of ancient Greek, so everyone starts with the same – equal – opportunities. And yet all pupils will find some points of recognition in relation to their own home language, which produces even more enthusiasm. It is amazing that our pupils can even write short sentences at the end of the project. It is also made more interesting for the pupils by not only focusing on the language itself: they enjoy the fascinating mythology and history. Their interest is not only stimulated by the different activating methods and ideas, but the enthusiasm of the student-teachers also has an enormous impact. Their curiosity for more turns out to be intense after the series of lessons.

Since I have a limited number of students who do the teacher training, I also put the didactic resources online in an editable format. This way, teachers who want to use the resources are able to do so. All teaching resources – currently in Dutch, with one course translated into

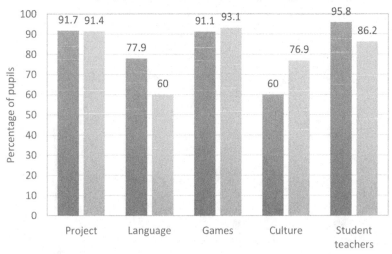

Figure 2.2 Percentage of positive pupil responses regarding aspects of the projects in Wales and the Flemish region.

English – can be found on the website: www.ancientgreeksyoungheroes.
ugent.be. It has been wonderful to see so many teachers adapt the
teaching resources to fit their own pupils' needs. Our project has even,
for the first time in Flemish educational history, enabled secondary
schools to offer ancient Greek to pupils who have not studied Latin
first, and more specifically to those pupils studying technical subjects
(in the so-called B-stream),[39] who would have otherwise never come
into contact with ancient Greek. Like the primary school pupils taking part in our project, these secondary school pupils also report enjoying the cognitive challenge which they do not normally get. The
project is clearly successful at raising aspirations among pupils from
deprived backgrounds. One teacher reports:

> The mix of theory and creative activities clearly appeals to pu-
> pils. Pupils especially appreciate that they can now do "something
> difficult". We can therefore certainly say that ancient Greek is a
> success with our pupils and the colleagues who teach it.

In this particular school, it was in fact not a classics teacher but a
French teacher who decided to teach ancient Greek to pupils of the
B-stream, which shows that lack of subject knowledge need not be a
barrier to teaching classics to non-traditional target groups. Through
the dissemination of didactic materials, the project has brought ancient
Greek to more than a thousand pupils in Flanders, though this likely
underestimates numbers, since many teachers are integrating didactic
materials in different subjects, such as history and modern languages.
The website gets hundreds of visitors each month, not only from
Europe and the US but also from other countries around the world.

2.2.3 *Aspirations and literacy: research findings*

The primary aim of *Young Heroes* is to support children growing up in
poverty by raising their academic self-confidence via the study of ancient Greek (hence classics as a 'tool'). For academic self-confidence,
as I argued in the previous chapter, tends to be lower among pupils
from deprived backgrounds. At the start of the project, the university
students who teach the lessons always run into the well-known stereotypes about ancient Greek: it is not for everyone, has no immediate
use, and is too difficult. Some pupils indicate in the first lesson that
ancient Greek is not for them, a teacher says that x or y will not be
able to do this, or pupils indicate that their parents do not understand
why they study this at school. Stereotypes are persistent,[40] but they do

not have to have negative consequences. By using these stereotypes to our advantage, the project works as a catalyst: not only is ancient Greek – throughout the five weeks of the project – revealed as a subject that *is* in fact accessible for these pupils, but the cognitive abilities of supposedly weaker pupils are also recognized within the school and home environments. Anecdotal teacher and student feedback tells us that pupils who were labelled 'weak' at the beginning of the lessons – whether by themselves or by a teacher – were seen to be blossoming and finding their voice by the end of the project. In this way, persistent negative labelling of certain pupils (whether by themselves or in their family or school environment) can be questioned and pupils' identity reframed in a more positive way.

While literacy is not the primary aim of the project, our lessons do increase pupils' literacy skills, as I learned from quantitative data analysis. In both 2019 and 2021, I tested pupils' spelling and reading comprehension before and after the project. I was able to examine the questionnaires of 44 out of 49 project pupils in both schools, a viable sample of 89.7% of the total group. The control group consisted of 20 pupils in School 2 who followed the regular curriculum. While the findings are provisional on account of the small sample size, they are nonetheless encouraging.[41]

Spelling of 20 Dutch words and questions on academic resilience were included in the baseline and post-test. No statistically significant result was achieved;[42] however, the project group slightly outperformed the control group. This in itself is a useful starting point for further research, particularly regarding the support the study of ancient Greek can provide to bolster pupils' mental resilience. Feedback from the student-teachers confirms this. One student-teacher said,

> What will stick with me most is that the most positive reactions came from the linguistically "weakest" pupils. Pupil X,[43] who is only in Belgium for the second year, wrote the most lines [in a specific exercise] of everyone. Pupil Y, whose teacher after the first lesson said she wouldn't be able to use the Greek alphabet, dared to raise her hand during discussions in the last lessons.

More success, however, came from comparing the reading-comprehension results of the project group with those of the control groups. I gave the pupils a short Dutch text on a Greek myth in both the baseline and post-test, with five content-related questions to answer about each. Pupils who had taken part in the project and had achieved similar reading-comprehension results to their peers before the project outperformed their peers statistically significantly after only approximately ten hours in five weeks of taking part in the project.[44] These results are wonderful, since they demonstrate the potential of the project. Since the surveys reveal no difference between children from a Flemish background and pupils from an ethnic minority background, the project is successful in its aim to reach pupils across ethnic and cultural barriers. There is one aspect of the project which requires development, and that is gender: in all parts of the test (reading comprehension, academic motivation, and spelling), boys tended to perform disproportionately less well than girls. Unfortunately, the gender gap is a well-known phenomenon in education,[45] so this is something I intend to work on in the future.

These test results echo results from the US primary school classics projects as well as evidence from UK projects, which I discussed above. While my foremost aim is to support pupils' quality of life, the quantitative data can help make the case for primary school classics among policymakers and school boards (more on this in Chapter 5). Ultimately, the strength of the project is that it allows for all pupils, regardless of their cognitive or linguistic ability or socioeconomic background, to feel heard and seen in ancient Greek lessons and to participate in knowledge creation, while also developing their literacy skills. One teacher we work with reported that pupils who participated in the project two years ago still acknowledge its value in their lives today, even though they are in fact studying technical subjects (B-stream) at secondary school level and will never again encounter ancient Greek in their studies. The project therefore not only adds quantitative but also long-term qualitative value to children's lives, far beyond the five lessons.

In short, pupil and teacher feedback suggests that the project functions as a (temporary) disruptor of the downward motivational spiral which pupils from deprived backgrounds tend to experience, while research findings corroborate that the project supports pupils' reading comprehension. The project demonstrates to both pupils and teachers that these children *are* able to deal with cognitively challenging subject matter. By changing stereotypical views about children growing up in poverty – their abilities, capabilities, and aspirations – the project is starting to function as a catalyst for social change. For this reason, in 2020, the project was awarded an annual prize for Science Communication by the Royal Flemish Academy of Belgium for Science and Arts.[46]

2.3 Good practice

While teaching classics at primary school is not a mainstream activity, my discussion of successful projects in the US and Europe attests to its social justice potential. What is clear, however, is that there is a huge variety of approaches to teaching classics at primary school. The majority of projects have taught or teach Latin while fewer offer Greek. Some projects are driven by primary school teachers themselves, sometimes in collaboration with other stakeholders, such as university staff or charities; yet secondary school teachers, volunteers, retirees, university students, and secondary school pupils also regularly act as teachers. The didactic approach varies hugely – from a focus on grammar via the reading-comprehension approach to a direct emphasis on literacy – primarily driven by the educational needs of local pupil groups, as well as the teachers' needs in integrating lessons into the curriculum. Finally, how much time is allocated for lessons also differs vastly. My own project takes one potential approach, chosen as much from necessity – limitations in time and number of student-teachers – as for pedagogical purposes. It is therefore useful to reflect on the various decisions educational practitioners have made over the past decades, in order to shape classics at primary school.

2.3.1 What do you mean by 'classics'?

First, whether you teach Latin or ancient Greek will depend not only on teacher expertise but also on interest and awareness by schools with which you might work. As I said before, Latin was successful at primary schools in Wales because it was linked with the social status of private schools. In the Flemish region, by contrast, Latin is less inaccessible, so the educational position of Greek *after* Latin makes it more aspirational. It is therefore important to reflect on what works in your specific context.

Before we design any Latin or ancient Greek course, it is also important to ask ourselves what our purpose is, what kind of 'classics' we are offering. Often, primary school classics is treated as the *prequel* of secondary school classics: the same didactic approach is used with more age-appropriate topics and activities. *Minimus*,[47] for example, takes a similar reading-comprehension approach to the popular secondary school Latin course *Cambridge Latin Course*,[48] and in the Italian version had more grammar added to prepare pupils for the more grammar-focused approach in Italian secondary schools.[49] Indeed, in order to make primary school pupils moving to secondary school aware of what classics is, offering Latin or Greek lessons will help them make a more informed decision. Increasingly popular communicative, 'active', or 'Living' approaches to Latin and ancient Greek teaching are now being used at primary school as well as secondary and university education, whether as main didactic approach or to complement the reading approach.[50] These are effective ways of teaching Latin or ancient Greek more inclusively than through the reading or grammar-translation approach only. Sometimes, Latin and Greek are also taught as remedial English at primary school. By teaching roots and derivations, disconnecting the Latin and Greek languages from their historical and cultural context, the Lexonik project, for instance, significantly increases children's English reading ability at primary and secondary school.[51] The Latin Programme also gets good results with an explicit focus on grammar in English and Latin.[52] Educators who are interested in focusing on short-term visible impact on pupils' metalinguistic awareness might be interested in this approach. In current practice, most primary schools that teach classics integrate some root teaching into their reading and/or communicative approach lessons.

Whether the learning objective of these approaches is for pupils to read texts, understand grammar, have conversations, understand derivations, learn about the culture and mythology, or – as is most prevalent – a combination of these, they all make it possible to teach classics inclusively, prepare pupils for secondary school, and improve pupils' literacy skills. However, none of these approaches necessarily work towards educational equity. Just as widening participation in classics by offering it at primary school does not necessarily work towards increased social justice, teaching classics inclusively does not entail working towards educational equity either. Teaching classics inclusively means all pupils in the classroom are engaged, while teaching towards social justice goes a step further. It requires pedagogy to be transformed, in order to empower pupils to disrupt destructive narratives about their abilities and chances in life. This necessitates a more radical reformulation of the concept of 'knowledge'. Because what do we consider to be knowledge of Latin or ancient Greek? Is it reading texts, memorizing words, understanding grammar, speaking the language – or should we redefine the concept of 'knowledge' entirely? In the *Young Heroes* courses, the answer to that question is yes: controversial though it may be, learning to read or speak either language is not the *main* aim. Indeed, considering the background of pupils as explained above, using the same approach as at secondary school would be counter-productive. I know this from experience: when my students and I first started teaching Latin, we wanted to use an existing coursebook to teach the language in a playful way; however, one of the teachers told me the English sentences were too difficult for the pupils and so we had to start from word level and build up metalinguistic awareness slowly, through phrases and sentences before we were able to address text level. This made me turn to Modern Foreign Language approaches to language learning, and I still apply these principles to *Young Heroes* today.[53]

It is important to clarify for yourself the aim of your lessons: is it to get more pupils to choose classics at secondary school, increase pupils' literacy or self-esteem, widen participation of classics by offering it to non-traditional target groups, or get pupils reading the beautiful stories from antiquity and its later tradition? All of these aims are equally valuable and can indeed be combined, but they cannot all be the *main* aim. If you want to get more pupils into classics at secondary school, it is important to offer them a realistic preview of what they might expect at secondary school – in our courses, by contrast, no vocabulary or grammar has to be memorized, which makes lessons more accessible but does not focus directly on the transition to secondary school.

2.3.2 Who would teach the course?

Secondly, the teacher of such a primary school classics course must be considered. In an ideal world, primary school teachers themselves would be able to teach some form of classics, and this is indeed what a number of innovative projects in the US did. It is also what a number of schools in the UK are now doing since Latin and ancient Greek can be integrated into the primary school curriculum,[54] and a number of schools in Flanders are also integrating the *Young Heroes* didactic material in lessons. However, this is still a minority: for many teachers, this is not realistically possible. Timetable restraints and lack of subject knowledge are given as understandable reasons against doing this. For those primary school teachers who are interested, there are ways around these arguments: classics can fit in nicely with learning objectives concerning, for example, literacy, foreign languages, or history, and teaching classics at primary school does not require a huge amount of in-depth subject knowledge. However, since teacher training is not widely available in most countries, collaboration with external interested stakeholders might support primary school teachers who want to offer some form of classics. This may also bring additional benefits.

In some projects, including my own, courses are taught by university students a concept called 'service education'. A major advantage is that students' relative closeness in age to the pupils and university-based status allow them to function as role models.[55] Letting students teach means I as coordinator can work with more schools than I would be able to, were I to teach the courses myself. I can create new teaching resources almost annually and keep the project going long term. There are of course drawbacks: mentoring teacher trainees is an intense and time-consuming activity for the coordinator, and as we ask class teachers to remain present during student-teacher lessons, the project requires active input from the school partners. As students are still training to be teachers there can be mistakes from time to time, and as student numbers tend to fluctuate from year to year, I am never 100% certain I will be able to offer lessons in our project schools – but that is why I keep the number of schools I work with in Flanders limited. Liz Butterworth (2017: 5–6) outlines further potential pitfalls of 'service education', arguing that it is possible to fall into the trap of wanting to 'help' rather than empower pupils, by sharing information that might be useful for their social context but in reality only confirms educational inequity. However, while the worst-case scenario leaves students with a 'misguided and inflated sense of their ability to address community needs', best practice equates to 'justice learning', which 'encourages students to recognize systemic injustice and direct their work towards long-term change'.[56] Rather than working *for* them in a top-down approach, working *with* schools, teachers, and pupils from the start in order to clarify their authentic needs means the worst-case scenario can be avoided and genuine empowerment and transformation can be facilitated for all those involved.[57] I agree with Steven Hunt (2022: 168) that ideally students supporting primary school teachers would be 'a step towards a more long-term solution, in which schools themselves take on the responsibility of teaching classical subjects'. I fear, however, that in most countries and contexts this is not a realistic prospect in the near or even long term. Since pupils testify to engaging with students not merely on a cognitive level but – more importantly – on an interpersonal level, and students tell me their teaching practice at secondary school is impacted positively by the teaching experience they have gained at the primary level, the benefits of school–university cooperation for widening participation in classics at primary school level seem to outweigh the disadvantages.

It is, however, also fairly common practice for secondary school teachers to go into a local primary school to teach classics, often to encourage pupils to sign up for courses in secondary school. As the example above of the French teacher teaching ancient Greek in the B-stream demonstrates, it is not necessary for teachers to have a strong classical training: many teachers learn Latin or ancient Greek alongside their pupils, which makes the discovery process of the language exciting for all. Other secondary school teachers do not do the teaching themselves, but train their final-year secondary school pupils to teach introductory Latin or Greek in a local primary school, and assess them on their teaching performance.[58] While the advantage, namely the relative closeness in age, is similar to student-teachers, such lessons cannot normally add up to a complete course owing to lack of timetabling space at secondary school. Nevertheless, I love this engagement of learners: this is certainly an option which will enthuse both the primary and secondary school pupils involved.

Finally, retirees and adult volunteers who have studied Latin or Greek earlier on in life are also well-known teacher options in primary school classics projects. This is in fact how Barbara Bell's inspiring course *Minimus* started in the UK,[59] and in contrast to the role model function of students, retirees may render the subject more accessible as they take on a non-academic mentoring role. It might in fact be possible to combine various teacher groups: at Swansea, at one point, I worked with student-teachers, volunteers, secondary school teachers, and a secondary school pupil who wanted to get involved – the Aequora project in the US and Barbara Bell's *Minimus* both work with similar diverse teacher groups.[60] Indeed, what all of these options demonstrate is that a successful format may bring stakeholders from different backgrounds together in the primary school environment, whether from universities, secondary schools, adult volunteers, or educational charities. In this way, no one has to reinvent the wheel or struggle on alone, and the experience is an enriching one for all. More about this in the final chapter.

2.3.3 What would be the course format?

Once you have decided who will teach the course, a decision needs to be made concerning the number and duration of lessons that will be taught. Ten hours per school year is what I am currently able to offer schools, on the basis of the students' workload as well as the schools' and university timetable. However, in the project I coordinated at Swansea University, we actually offered Latin and ancient Greek throughout the school year, which allowed us to make more headway with regard to grammar and thematic exploration than we are currently able to. In a review of 100 years of research concerning the impact of classics teaching on pupils, it appeared 20 minutes per day might be optimal,[61] but this is no doubt unrealistic for most teachers. Since the short *Young Heroes* course of 5 two-hour lessons already causes an increase in reading comprehension, however, one hour per week throughout an entire term should reveal further tangible benefits. If in doubt, I would suggest starting small, so you can find out what works for both you and the pupils.

As this section has demonstrated, there is no one approach to teaching Latin or ancient Greek at primary school. This means various projects may be struggling independently in their endeavour to keep lessons going, but lack of government guidelines and space in the curriculum also means that classics can be taught in a relatively stress-free context, without the pressure of achievement with which it is often associated secondary school. There are many decisions to be made by anyone interested in starting a course at primary school, but getting interested stakeholders from various educational contexts together can be exciting and inspiring for all involved parties.

2.4 Conclusion and reflection tools

This chapter has discussed how widening participation in classics might be achieved at primary school. A discussion of past and present projects reveals not only the rich variety of possible formats, all with their advantages and disadvantages, but also the quantitative and qualitative impact of such projects on pupils. This demonstrates the enormous potential of teaching classics at primary school, as it may be incorporated into the curriculum in many different ways, to different ends.

On the basis of this discussion about the various formats of classics at primary school, I would now invite you to reflect on your current – or potentially future – practice (Table 2.1). The answer categories have the same key as in Chapter 1:

- − −   This is definitely not a priority for me.
- −   I pay attention to this from time to time.
- − +   I would like to pay more attention to this, but I'm not sure how.
- +   I regularly pay attention to this.
- + +   This is an integral part of my current thinking.

Table 2.1 Reflection tools

	− −	−	− +	+	+ +
I know of others already teaching Latin or Greek at primary school in my country or area.					
I can see how classics might contribute to the needs of pupils in my country or area.					
I understand the difference between merely widening participation in classics by teaching it at primary school, and teaching it to work towards social justice.					
I am aware of the potential benefits of primary school pupils studying Latin or ancient Greek, at the level of literacy as well as aspirations.					

If I were to offer classics at primary school, this is how I would define it.

If I were to offer classics at primary school, this is who would teach it. (Why are they a suitable teacher for the particular school group you have in mind?)

If I were to offer classics at primary school, this is the number and duration of lessons I would opt for.

Notes

1 School District of Philadelphia 1970: 12.
2 Kitchell 2014, Bracey 2017.
3 Sussman 1978: 351.
4 Mavrogenes 1977, Sussman 1978.
5 Mavrogenes 1977: 268.
6 School District of Philadelphia 1970: 1.
7 Mavrogenes 1977: 270.
8 Mavrogenes 1977: 272.
9 Mavrogenes 1977: 270.
10 School District of Philadelphia 1970: 12. Emphasis in the original.
11 School District of Philadelphia 1970: 1.
12 Bracke & Bradshaw 2020: 239.
13 Bracke & Bradshaw 2020: 123.
14 LeBovit 1967, Cederstrom 1974, Masciantonio 1975, Sheridan 1976, Fromchuck 1984, Bassman & Ironsmith 1984, Polsky 1986, Sienkewicz et al. 2004.

15 George 1998: 230–31.
16 Butterworth 2017: 3.
17 http://www.ascaniusyci.org/about.htm.
18 Maguire 2018.
19 Bell 1999 and 2004 are good starting points. See Bell & Wing-Davey 2018: 111–16.
20 http://irisproject.org.uk/index.php/the-iris-project/iris-project-history and https://www.thelatinprogramme.co.uk/; for the Latin Programme, see Bell & Wing-Davey 2018: 117–27.
21 Bracke 2015 and 2016.
22 England: Wardle 2021; Wales: Hwb 2022 and my invited reports: Bracke 2015a; Bracke 2017a.
23 https://classicsforall.org.uk/my-school-wants-classics/resources-0/key-stage-1-2-resources.
24 Robinson 2013, 2016, 2017.
25 https://hands-up-education.org/primarylatin.html.
26 Northumbria University Newcastle 2015, Bell & Wing-Davey 2018: 120–21, Holmes-Henderson 2023.
27 https://classicsforall.org.uk/why-support-us/our-impact.
28 Duchemin, Durand, Franceschetti 2023, Nausicaa 2015. *Eurêka* is another French project, based in Paris. See https://eureka-paris5.fr.
29 The Netherlands: Rosings 2023; Greece: https://ellinikiagogi.gr/?lang=en. See https://www.euroclassica.eu/portale/euroclassica/links/courses-didactics/latin-greek-at-primary-school.html.
30 Bracke 2016.
31 Lahaye 2019; Chapter 1, pp. 3–4.
32 Chapter 1, p. 12; Goosen et al. 2017: 113–14.
33 Rosiers 2021. See Woolard 2021: 12 on linguistic authority of dominant and dominated groups.
34 Van Avermaet et al. 2015.
35 https://www.oudegriekenjongehelden.ugent.be/en/teaching-materials/course-1-monsters-in-storytelling-traditions/lesson-5-a-heros-journey/.
36 Questionnaires were gathered in 2019, 2021, and 2022 (not in 2020 as the project was cut short because of the COVID-19-related lockdown). A total of 109 pupils filled in the questionnaires. While these figures are very good, they are skewed by the figures from 2021 which were slightly lower than usual. Student-teachers were not allowed to move in between pupils or bring them to the front of the class, which somewhat inhibited our usual didactic approach, and one of the schools again moved to online lessons. If we only consider 2019 and 2022, the percentage of pupils who circled the 'happy emoji' in response to questions is 91.4% for the project as a whole, 60% for learning of new words, 76.9% for culture and myth, 93.1% for playing games, and 86.2% for student engagement, which is up to 8% higher than the figures which include the COVID-19 year. It does demonstrate that, in spite of the COVID-19 measures pupils and students had to adhere to in schools, enjoyment of the project was still high.
37 The joy conveyed by pupils resembles the findings of Butterworth (2017: 4) regarding the Aequora project.
38 For this comparison I removed the figures from COVID-19 year 2021, n. 36.
39 Chapter 1, p. 12.

40 I discuss potential responses to such biased objections in Chapter 5.
41 All test results were analysed using the two-sided Mann–Whitney U test.
42 $p = 0.11; d = 0.43$.
43 Name removed for anonymity.
44 $p = 0.002; d = 0.56$.
45 Derks & Vermeersch 2001, Smith 2016.
46 See https://www.kvab.be/nl/prijzen/jaarprijzen-wetenschapscommunicatie.
47 See p. 26.
48 See https://www.clc.cambridgescp.com/.
49 Bell & Wing-Davey 2018: 113.
50 Hunt 2021.
51 Northumbria University Newcastle 2015. See also Holmes & Keffer 2010.
52 Bell & Wing-Davey 2018.
53 See the 'eclectic' Modern Foreign Language approach to teaching Latin at secondary school, discussed by Hunt 2021.
54 Maguire 2018.
55 Bracke 2016.
56 Butin 2007.
57 More on the advantages and pitfalls of 'service education', Butterworth 2017 and Caterine 2018.
58 Bell & Wing-Davey 2018: 114 for a British example, Rosings 2023 for a Dutch example.
59 Bell & Wing-Davey 2018.
60 Butterworth 2017: 5.
61 Bracke & Bradshaw 2020.

3 Six steps to transformative learning through classics at primary school

3.1 Classics and disorientation in the primary classroom

In Chapter 1, we explored how educational inequity functions and where the study of classics fits into the system. The end of that chapter presented examples of innovative work being done to improve access to classics in secondary schools, by reformulating the subject's target group, definitions, and functions. Chapter 2 similarly explored how participation in classics has been expanded at the level of primary education in various countries. Now we know our target group/s and which practical questions to consider when setting up a project at primary school level, we can start reflecting on actual classroom practice: how can we engage with pupils through classics in a way that will empower them from a social justice perspective? To answer this question, we need to start from pupils' lived experiences.

3.1.1 The challenges of multidiversity

My project's target group are children growing up in deprived circumstances, but it is of course possible to engage with any social group in a primary school – indeed not every pupil in our class groups belongs to our precise target group. However, whether you work largely with disadvantaged pupils or a socially diverse group, with cognitively differentiated or strong pupils, children's lived experiences vary dramatically. This is the case because diversity does not just depend on social factors such as class, ethnicity, or residential location, just as I discussed in Chapter 1 regarding multidimensional poverty. Diversity is a complex reality which exists at the level of both group and individual differences, and entails 'gender, sexual orientation, age, physical and mental faculties, class, language, education level, religion, ideology, societal structures', and more.[1] This means that no two pupils in any

DOI: 10.4324/9781003229742-3

given classroom live the same lives. It is not necessarily the case that white *plus* male *plus* cis-gender *plus* hetero *plus* affluent *equals* wholly privileged. But it does mean it is likely that visible and invisible social barriers restrict some children's access to socioeconomically and culturally valued goods less than others. Marginalization, on the other hand, has a tendency to become more severe when it is experienced at the junctions of several of these identity differences. Indeed, 'intersecting vulnerabilities can create life deprivations that are greater than the sum of other single factors'.[2] Studies have long demonstrated that discrimination experienced by black women, for example, amounts to a unique form of marginalization which is not merely the sum of *gender plus race*.[3] Even in a seemingly socially homogeneous classroom, different lived experiences are thus at play. The complex manifestations of privilege and deprivation which arise on the basis of these combined factors are called 'multidiversity'.[4]

Taking the multidiverse needs of individual pupils into account seems like a gargantuan task for any teacher: how do you ensure that all pupils – regardless of their lived experience at the levels of ethnicity, class, gender, religion, and all other factors mentioned above – feel seen and heard in classics lessons in terms of content, didactics, and assessment? In practice, reaching all pupils in a multidiverse classroom is often difficult and frustrating. Multidiversity is a reality that originates outside the school gates, but harmony is often difficult to achieve or maintain in our rapidly evolving society: identity differences between social groups can lead to polarizing conflicts. Although these identity differences originate outside the school gates, they resonate loudly at school and have a tangible impact on teachers and pupils. Both come to the classroom with an identity based on multidiverse factors, many of which they are not aware of. For not only do our conscious thoughts and actions define our behaviour, but unconscious bias does as well.[5] The human brain is equipped to analyze situations slowly and come to a nuanced understanding, but also tends to make instant and usually binary judgements, especially when under pressure: same or other, good or bad.[6] 'Confirmation bias' (looking for confirmation of information you already possess about others, be it positive or negative), 'beauty bias' (some people are afforded more status because they are better looking), the 'halo effect' (good impressions of others have an effect on how we treat them), and 'similarity attraction' (people are naturally inclined to like those who resemble themselves more than those who do not) are all part of human nature and have an impact on how both pupils and teachers handle classroom situations.

Raised with limiting beliefs and biases regarding their cognitive capacities and identity, pupils from disadvantaged backgrounds are much more susceptible to falling into a downward spiral of demotivation as I discussed in Chapter 1, while pupils' surroundings (teachers, parents, school boards, etc.) run the risk of acquiring a fixed notion of a pupil's capacities too. In order to disrupt this destructive narrative, it is not sufficient to merely offer pupils a new challenge, such as teaching them Latin or ancient Greek (i.e. widen participation in classics), though that is certainly an important step.[7] It is vital that we also adapt pedagogy so it at least facilitates pupils' reflection on this narrative and offers them the potential for metacognitive growth and transformation.

3.1.2 Classics and the 'zone of optimal confusion'[8]

Adapting pedagogy is not an easy task, as it means the standard curriculum cannot be maintained. However, in order to encourage pupils (gently, carefully, and appropriately) to reflect on the damaging narratives which shape their lives and futures, I would argue Jack Mezirow's 1991 concept of 'transformative learning' offers a useful framework with which to think. Mezirow's original theory was designed for adult and young adult education, but it has since been used to further pedagogy in other educational contexts, such as second language learning and intercultural competence.[9] Mezirow (1991: 5) argues that we all work with taken-for-granted frames of reference

> which selectively shape and delimit expectations, perceptions, cognition, and feelings. They set our "line of action." Once set, we automatically move from one specific activity (mental or behavioral) to another. We have a strong tendency to reject ideas that fail to fit our preconceptions, labeling those ideas as unworthy of consideration – aberrations, nonsense, irrelevant, weird, or mistaken.

These frames of reference also shape the identities of the pupils with whom I work. Disrupting the downward spiral of demotivation can therefore only be done by disrupting this frame of reference which shapes their (and our) lives. Indeed, according to Mezirow (1991: 5), '[w]hen circumstances permit, transformative learners move toward a frame of reference that is more inclusive, discriminating, self-reflective, and integrative of experience'. The catalyst of this process is what Mezirow calls a 'disorienting experience' or dilemma: a situation that challenges our current belief system. Most people, when confronted with a 'disorienting' situation, understandably choose to ignore it and return to their known frame of reference. However, when a 'disorienting' experience is strong enough, it cannot be ignored, and a metacognitive process (i.e. thinking about thinking and learning) starts. First you start reflecting on what just happened and assess your held beliefs which are being challenged. You relate your current disorientation to the experiences of others and start exploring new beliefs and planning actions that may better suit your needs. You gather knowledge to implement these new beliefs and experiment. By practising new beliefs in different circumstances, self-confidence grows and this new perspective can be integrated into your life.

This is Mezirow's theory in a nutshell – there are variations, but the key phase in the process is the disorienting dilemma, as this is where a choice must be made to either ignore the disorientation and maintain the – in the case of the pupils with whom I work damaging – self-beliefs, or accept the challenge of reflection and explore alternatives. In the primary classroom, I would argue that not every step in Mezirow's process is explicitly visible, but nevertheless pupils of that age are perfectly capable – as I have experienced – of transforming certain beliefs, especially about limitations they believed define them. In fact, as I said in the previous chapter, at the end of each course, not only pupils but also teachers are surprised by pupils' constructive engagement with the challenge that is ancient Greek.

For some pupils, only some activities the course offers are disorienting. However, for many, the entire course is one big disorienting dilemma: sometimes parents are against it, sometimes the teacher is reluctant, their peers do not understand it, or they themselves find the activities challenging. Inevitably, questions arise for the pupil: am I good enough to do Greek/Latin/classics? What does this course mean to me? How do I integrate this into my world view – and indeed *should* I integrate this? Some pupils, confronted with a disorienting dilemma, will resist and maintain their world view – and I certainly do not want to force any changes. However, through the steps I will describe below, it is possible to guide pupils, as carefully as possible, in examining their world view, recognizing its limitations, exploring alternatives, and perhaps even adapting their world view to integrate the newly acquired insights and acting accordingly. Rather than an end in itself, language learning in this context also becomes a transformative tool for social justice, inviting pupils to reflect critically on identity, both theirs and another's.

There is, however, a delicate balance to be struck. While some scholars argue that 'the shocking and sudden critical event' is most significant for effective transformative learning,[10] others warn that 'the trick with designing a disorienting dilemma is that it has to be unsettling enough to shake students out of the comfort zone, but not so discomforting that those students will do their best to avoid dealing with it'.[11] Sidney D'Mello and Arthur Graesser (2014: 299) call this the 'zone of optimal confusion'. Much in fact depends on the teacher. As Kashi Raj Pandey (2021: 7) argues, 'the way a teacher perceives her/ himself, whether as a facilitator, artist, or educator, plays a transformative role in the classroom'. When a disorienting experience strikes the right balance, it can work brilliantly to empower pupils to disrupt their own narrative, but for any teacher, getting this right entails a huge learning curve. Even with the best intentions to empower pupils, a teacher may design an activity which works brilliantly for some pupils yet is confrontational for (and rejected or evaded by) others. In that case, it is up to the teacher to reflect and experiment in order to find that right balance. This is what I mean when I say that teaching for multidiversity is a gargantuan task. To clarify what might have seemed somewhat abstract so far, I want to share with you three (luckily rare) incidents from my own primary school experiences which did not offer a balanced disorientating experience, from which I will extract six practical 'steps' which may support future transformative learning practice.

3.1.3 Example 1: a lack of disorientation

Ten years ago, when my students first starting teaching Latin in a primary school in Wales, we created a craft activity whereby pupils were allowed to create and decorate either shields or jewellery. I had designed it as a break in between linguistic exercises: pupils were allowed to choose from the two activities, and holding true to binary gender stereotyping, boys chose shields while girls chose jewellery. Pupils had a great time and the teacher worked with them to finish their craft activities after the lesson was done. Afterwards, I pondered pupils' voluntary binary segregation with my students, since we had in fact wanted to avoid gender stereotyping by allowing pupils to choose their own activity. Where did we go wrong? In hindsight, it is clear that we activated and validated the binary gender norms with which pupils were growing up themselves. We had not offered a disorienting experience, but a binary gendered activity which responds more to modern gender stereotypes than to the historical reality of antiquity, when men of a higher social class wearing jewellery was the norm and some women took an active part in war, even if Romans generally considered those women unnatural.[12]

The result was a 'fun activity' enjoyed by all but largely meaningless. One way to render the activity more meaningful would be to add contextualization: instead of presenting the activity as a crafts moment to offer a break during a linguistic lesson, it would be more meaningful to integrate the activity into the actual cultural learning of the lesson. I would ask the pupils which activity they would like to choose and why, thus prompting a discussion of pupils' own gendered expectations and how these might have been experienced in the ancient world more broadly than 'Rome'. In fact, we went further than gender stereotyping: by silently validating that 'Roman boys' would engage with shields and 'Roman girls' with jewellery, we also generalized at a level of class, age, and social status, as if *all* Roman women wore the same elaborate attire while *all* men had a shield. You might argue that the exercise might better be replaced with a non-stereotyped activity, and that is of course an option. However, by framing it with an age-appropriate discussion about social difference and its implications, the same activity might be retained and applied for pupils to gain meaningful insights regarding important intersections of class and gender in antiquity and today and, importantly, reflect on their own binary gender stereotypes. By using examples from antiquity, it is possible for children to arrive at understanding of difference inductively and intuitively.

This activity was only an issue for the students and myself: the pupils and teacher had engaged constructively, and pupil feedback was incredibly positive: they loved the craft activities. More difficult, however, are moments when well-intentioned activities accidentally trigger pupils. The following example is one which took me a number of years to come to terms with.

3.1.4   Example 2: finding a balanced disorientation

In one of the first Latin lessons I ever devised at Swansea, pupils were taught about Roman gods: in order to practise nominative noun endings (for example, Minerva or Mercurius),[13] they were asked to make up and draw their own god and give them an imaginative name with either the masculine or feminine ending. The first time a pupil told me their religion forbade them from drawing a god, I was stunned. In my zeal and ignorance, I felt the pupil was bringing non-classroom-related issues around religion and culture into the classroom. With other pupils trying to get my attention, I explained to the pupil that it was 'just' an exercise and moved on when they refused to take part. I'm still embarrassed when I think of my response at the time, which invalidated the pupil's lived experience.

The second time I was confronted with a pupil who rejected this exercise on religious grounds, a few years later, I had spent some time reflecting on it and had come to the conclusion that an alternative exercise was the answer. However, when I suggested to the pupil they draw a hero instead, they did not understand how that was any better. I despairingly suggested – flummoxed as other pupils wanted my attention – they 'just draw something else'. The wrong response, again. My frustration lingered, and I decided to prepare an alternative activity entirely. Armed with a short text about the gods and some questions for pupils to answer, I triumphantly placed it in front of the third pupil who rejected the activity, two years later. However, since the text was not discussed or contextualized in class, there was no real point, and both the pupil and I came away from the lesson frustrated. I think it is because it seemed like a 'nice introductory activity' that I did not question the educational value of 'drawing your own god', even when challenged. At the time I had not thought about disorienting experiences, but it is clear this activity was too confrontational for some pupils while it meant very little for others, so it did not offer a balanced disorienting experience. I eventually decided to get rid of the exercise altogether, though only after three pupils had rejected the activity on separate occasions. Lesson learnt: sometimes, rather than persevering in applying or adapting an activity, as a teacher you need to admit when an activity does not function as a valuable learning tool.

Fast-forward a few more years: as part of a workshop on ancient Greek magic, I had decided to get pupils to create an ancient curse tablet, write some Greek phrases on it, and draw an ancient demon, just like on some existing curse tablets.[14] Sure enough, one of the pupils told me they were not allowed to draw a demon (or indeed create the curse tablet) on religious grounds. I could weep: I had fallen into the same trap yet again. However, this was not just a 'just-make-it-up' exercise like drawing your own god. The entire workshop had been about ancient curse tablets and the creative activity had been integrated fully. After our theoretical discussion, I asked pupils why they thought they were going to be creating their own curse tablet on aluminium foil. This turned out to be a difficult question: pupils thought it was just some creative fun, or for practising their Greek. They were keen to get started, but I stopped them, and we debated the primary objective of the exercise, namely to confront them with the darkness and other-ness of the ancient Greeks by going through the ritual of writing the curse, drawing the demons, folding the aluminium foil, and stabbing through it. Most pupils do not learn much about ancient magic, and when they do, it is usually with references to stories about Circe or Medea which, though ghastly, are mythological.[15] Confrontation with the gruesome historical reality of magic is rare. Having to create their own curse tablet integrates Object-Based Learning, since pupils are invited to interrogate the object as well as conceptualize their thinking about it and the context in which it was created and used.[16] When the pupil stated their objections to the exercise, I told them they could choose to do an alternative exercise, but asked if they had understood the purpose of this activity. The pupil took one look around the classroom and started on the exercise – I was amazed. Of course they were influenced by their peers who were excitedly taking part, but this was no different from previous years when pupils had rejected the activity, so I feel the contextualization of the activity also made a difference. The pupil had understood the learning objective: they were not asked or forced to go against their religious beliefs, but invited to engage in an object-based experiment. I would never want pupils to get into trouble at home or in their social group because of activities in which they take part in my lessons. However, if an exercise invites them to broaden their boundaries just a little, I would argue that is a balanced disorienting experience worth having. After the activity, I asked the entire class how they felt about creating an ancient Greek curse tablet. Answers ranged from 'weird' and 'funny' to 'disturbing', 'disgusting', and 'creepy', after which we discussed why they would feel like that. What pupils described is essentially an experience of cognitive dissonance, experienced by going through the motions of creating an ancient curse while sitting in modern classroom, which broadened their understanding of antiquity, and potentially their own beliefs.

You may argue that the exercise should be avoided since it is triggering for pupils from particular religious and cultural backgrounds. However, I would argue the disorienting experience offered to pupils in this exercise is balanced and has an object-based learning objective. For this reason, I value this particular exercise as a learning tool. While my pupils no longer draw gods, I have also adapted this exercise in other courses: in the course my students teach about ancient Greek monsters, pupils draw a monstrous self-portrait which provokes much enthusiasm and no objections (see Chapter 4). I feel the initial activity has now been adapted to a more useful learning objective, namely allowing pupils to reflect on self and other/the monstrous. Keeping that fine line between supporting and challenging pupils is, however, not easy to get right.

3.1.5 Example 3: a disorientation of pain[17]

If these two activities were uncomfortable to teach and reflect on, other issues are outright painful. Please note I merely mention the specific ethnic details in the following incident to make a point about the materialization of ethnicity-based conflict in the classroom, not as a generalization of specific minority groups. In one of everyone's favourite lessons taught in the *Young Heroes* project, pupils connect words for family connections (father, mother, child, …) in various European languages, and add the respective words from their own home languages (see Figure 3.1).[18] The whole class then discusses differences and parallels between languages, with the aim of fostering community in the Flemish educational context in which home languages are not always positively integrated.[19] Pupils tend to start this exercise with hesitation but find their curiosity about language activated as they go on: a well-balanced discomforting experience – normally.

About a year ago, an incident occurred when one child stated Kurdish as home language: a child from a different background in that region responded that Kurdish is not a language and that, since Kurds

Figure 3.1 Pupils connect words for family connections in various European languages, also adding their own languages.

don't have a country, they should not be allowed to exist. This is clearly a painful discriminatory issue at the intersections of language, ethnicity, and culture that was brought into the classroom from the child's experiences outside school. Even though the child cannot be blamed for holding these beliefs, it is important to call out discrimination in the classroom. At the time, unfortunately, both the class teacher and my students were shocked into silence, and nobody responded. I was disappointed in myself since I had not anticipated this, and as we were busily preparing for the next lessons, I forgot to follow it up. Lesson learned: after this, I spent a lot of time thinking how I would respond were a similar incident ever to occur – and I found it challenging to anticipate. Since then, I have done research on conflict transformation and discuss it with my students before they start teaching. The reality is that transformative learning involves questioning strict boundaries and differences while creating broader connections, which can cause tension and discomfort for some participants. Retaining that space of discomfort and disorientation is challenging for even the most experienced teacher. Nevertheless, it is important to anticipate this and be prepared not to freeze when confrontational moments occur.[20]

This was one of the most painful moments of my primary school experience, but needless to say, I have experienced more moments in my teaching career when I did not assess a disorienting experience accurately, because I was stuck in my own bias, unaware of the pupil's lived experience, overwhelmed, tired, or distracted. Teaching for social justice requires a lot of active reflection and self-awareness on the teacher's behalf. Even then, some biases or conflicts that go beyond the classroom can only be acknowledged, not resolved. It is not possible for any teacher to undo all of the biases which children pick up outside the classroom – but we can start working on them and indeed on our own. Making mistakes is inevitable, and it is important to be kind to ourselves. It is therefore useful to think of transformative learning as a process, not a specific point in time to reach, since no class group is ever entirely alike. In the words of bell hooks (1994: 11): 'Teaching is a performative act... [O]ur work ... is meant to serve as a catalyst that calls everyone to become more and more engaged, to become active participants in learning.'

These examples demonstrate that creating a balanced disorienting experience for pupils is not straightforward. I have extracted six steps from the above reflection which may facilitate transformative learning for primary school pupils by means of classics. Being aware of these steps may help others avoid falling into the pitfalls I have exemplified. Some of these steps might be obvious to you, others a step too far.

I would encourage you to reflect on which step might possibly feel right to take, taking your workload and well-being into account. Teaching for social justice may be painful at times for both teacher and pupils, but taking just one small step as a teacher can make a big difference in enabling hook's 'catalyst' in young people's lives and indeed our own.

3.2 'This pedagogy will be made and remade'[21]

In a discussion about pedagogy for social justice, four aspects of teaching must be addressed. I have already addressed the first aspect, namely the target group, in Chapters 1 and 2 when I discussed widening participation in classics. In the rest of this chapter, I will therefore focus on the remaining three aspects, namely content, didactic approach, and assessment.[22]

3.2.1 Step 1: backward design

When designing a new curriculum, it is traditional to start from the vocabulary, grammar, texts, or myths you would like your pupils to come into contact with, find a reasonable assessment, and then consider how you might make this inclusive. What is called 'backward design' moves transformative learning and social justice from being an afterthought to the core of the curriculum design process: starting from your pupils' multidiverse needs, you then develop content, didactic method, and a broad assessment which allow you to develop your social justice learning outcomes.[23] Most countries now have learning objectives which aim to guide schools in teaching pupils about multidiversity – whether they are labelled diversity, inclusivity, citizenship, intercultural competence, or something similar – and in order to fit your curriculum into its local educational system, you might want to see which learning objectives would genuinely be of use to you and your pupils.[24] In the Flemish context, this means I take into account 'social skills' learning objectives concerning 'respect and appreciation for others' (1.2), 'admitting being in the wrong, listening to criticism and learning from it' (1.9), and 'cooperating with others regardless of social background, gender, or ethnicity' (3).[25]

However, classics teaching for social justice goes beyond learning outcomes; it also aims to act as a catalyst to enact change. To that end, my students and I put together our courses based on the intersections of ethnicity, class, and language as key problem areas in mind, using ancient Greek as a bridge between children's various backgrounds. The main learning objective for each course is activating learning about language and culture which enables children to grow and potentially transform destructive narratives about self and other. The second, connected, learning objective is raising pupils' metacognitive and metalinguistic awareness, i.e. reflection on learning (and) languages. Teaching pupils about ancient Greek words, linguistic structures, texts, stories, and derivations is done to achieve those ends. In that context, we have created courses on 'identity', 'a journey through ancient Greece', and 'monsters in storytelling traditions'.

However, it is not necessary to make ethnicity and class the focus of any course. Recently, colleagues and students from Leiden and Ghent Universities and the National Museum of Antiquities in Leiden (the Netherlands) worked with me to create online ancient Greek learning resources using museum objects. Since our target group was bigger and even more diverse than usual – we wanted to reach *any* Flemish and Dutch 10- to 12-year-old children through online lessons – we decided to focus on the topic 'fact and fiction', using stories and objects from antiquity to help children explore the ambiguity of digital technology and social media.[26] It is only after deciding on the aims – and indeed the *main* aim – of the course with regard to multidiverse needs of our particular pupils, and reflecting on which learning objectives (both within the curriculum and our own social justice agenda) might fit our purpose, that the ancient Greek part of our course is developed. The next steps will give further information on how content, didactic approach, and assessment might be developed in this context.

3.2.2 Step 2: broadening the canon for local teaching

Much work has been done to broaden what we mean by classics or antiquity already,[27] so I will keep this section short. I already discussed in Chapter 1 the fact that neither knowledge nor pedagogy is ideologically neutral.[28] Teaching about language and culture specifically implies you will pass on your personal language ideology, namely your own opinions and ideas, to your pupils: about the definition and status of any particular language and culture, for example, or which authorities to follow concerning 'correct' language usage. It is on the basis of these beliefs about classics that a canon of knowledge came into being throughout the centuries, which has shifted as the need arose. Texts and stories read at secondary school, the great figures from classical antiquity, and Latin and Greek grammar, which tend to make an appearance at secondary school, are valuable and can be exciting, but it is important not to romanticize this canonical knowledge. In the words of Sarah E. Bond (2019), the classroom canons we present to our students during the short [time] that we have their attention are often an intellectual sculpture; one composed of stones quarried from what we were taught and what we have now deemed important to know. We can't introduce our students to every marble ever made, but we can present an admittedly synthetic but more inclusive structure to them of what classical antiquity was through our syllabi.

But how do you do this at primary school where most children hardly know anything about the Greeks? The first step is broadening our definition of antiquity from the start, geographically beyond Italy and Greece (and Europe), historically beyond 800 BC to 476 CE, linguistically beyond Latin and Greek, and conceptually beyond the 'Greeks' and 'Romans'. This seems like a huge task, yet it can start with small steps: geographically, you can adapt maps so they do not (only) show Europe or the southern Mediterranean but take a broader view. We now, for example, start our courses with a map of the continents, which we use to discuss with pupils their own backgrounds and ancient Greece's strategic position on the boundary of three continents. By defining the Greeks not (only) as starting point of the European or Mediterranean tradition but as a link on busy trading routes between continents, children are immediately invited to view ancient Greece as a broader concept. If you introduce this viewpoint of antiquity at the start of the course, it is important to maintain it throughout. In the online course on 'fact and fiction' which I just mentioned, this means Egyptian and Near Eastern objects are used alongside typically Greek and Roman objects: a Greco-Roman *syrinx*, for example, is introduced alongside an Egyptian harp in an object-based lesson about music.[29] As long as the use of these objects is clearly introduced and they are put into context, this increases the accessibility of the course.

Conceptually, we also no longer use gender and ethnic stereotypes in the images accompanying the course. For a long time, exactly which images my students used in their PowerPoints was something I overlooked – with focus on the creation of weekly lessons, it seemed of secondary importance. It was only through the years that my concerns about the stereotypical nature of some drawings of ancient Greek children or gods we were using crystallized. I started going through our didactic materials to replace stereotypical images with more appropriate and historically correct ones.[30] Stereotypical (white) images of gods, represented in LEGO figurines, for example, were replaced by more nuanced images drawn by a student specifically for our course (Figure 3.2); gender and racially stereotyped images of boys and girls

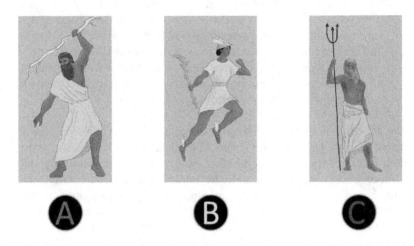

Figure 3.2 'Inclusive' drawings of ancient Greek gods created by a student specifically for our current courses.

replaced by more accurate and nuanced presentations. This is not an easy job, but you might, for example, get your pupils involved and get them to make more appropriate drawings which may be added to future PowerPoints or handouts.

It may seem contradictory to 'broaden' the curriculum in order to teach 'locally', but it is precisely this broadened view of antiquity which allows for pupils from different contexts to feel they have a voice in the exploration of antiquity. This emphasizes the point I made earlier, that there is no 'one size fits all' approach to teach classics as a tool for social justice at primary school, since the multidiverse needs of pupils need to be taken into account. For multidiversity teaching, broadening the curriculum is thus a key step – but not the only one.

3.2.3 Step 3: deepening learning from 5Fs to 3Ps

The next step is reflecting on the way in which we give shape to this broadened view of antiquity. Teaching about other languages and cultures is often anchored in what are called 'the five F's': Food, Fashion, Famous people, Festivals, and Flags (with Folk dance and Fairs sometimes replacing others). Indeed, what the Romans or Greeks ate, wore, or did at religious festivals, as well as the lives of famous authors and public figures, is valuable information covered in many classics courses. However, these 5Fs are only the visible tip of the cultural iceberg and if these aspects are prioritized, the risk is that pupils will primarily acquire static and possibly stereotypical knowledge of ancient culture and language. Integrating less visible aspects of culture, so-called 'deep culture', is possible by shifting the focus from the 5Fs to the 3Ps: Practices, Products, and Perspectives.[31] Practices are forms of behaviour which people exhibit within and between groups. This can include expected behaviour between masters and slaves, gender roles, rites of passage connected to birth, marriage, or death, and others. In order to find out about Practices in antiquity, we can examine Products, which are both the material and immaterial creations of any given culture, such as pottery, temple remains, toys, or texts (material), or stories, music, or laws (immaterial). Both Practices and Products are, however, shaped by Perspectives, meaning the values and beliefs a certain social group or society holds.

Applying this approach to language and culture teaching is less abstract than it appears. In lesson 3 of the 'Fact and fiction' course, for example, pupils learn about animals in antiquity. However, rather than offering a static image (Product) of what an animal is, different objects of not only 'real' animals (such as the horse, bull, or dog) but also hybrid mythological animals (such as the griffins) and hybrid human-animals (such as the sphinx) are juxtaposed. Doing different exercises on all of these can tease out awareness among pupils on the ways in which the ancient Greeks thought about 'humans' and 'animals', and particularly the boundaries and fluidity between these identities (Practice). By inviting pupils to think about these Products and Practices, they can come to an understanding not only about the Greeks' conceptualization of self and other, but also about the present impact of certain social media filters – which allow people to superimpose, for example, animal features onto their face – on our own notions of identity (Perspectives). The static, more superficial, and stereotypical image of animals versus humans is thus reformulated in a more nuanced manner, in order to make children more aware of their own daily Products (apps and mobile phone), Practices (e.g. adapting settings on selfies), and Perspectives (how do I present myself to others in a digital age?).

Bringing attention to cultural Practices and Perspectives through Products is of key importance when teaching multidiverse groups of pupils, because as teachers, we operate from our own background and thereby spotlight our own culture's (and language's) Perspectives and

Practices without even thinking about it. However, as John Uzo Ogbu (1988: 13) argued,

> cultural tasks vary from culture to culture because different populations have worked out different solutions to common problems in life, such as how to make a living, reproduce, maintain order within their border, defend themselves against outsiders, and so on.

Formulating the ancient Greeks or Romans not as static entities but societies with dynamic, complicated, contradictory, and evolving Practices, Products, and Perspectives means not one particular solution to a cultural task – or one child's cultural background – is presented as being superior to another. It can be as simple as asking pupils to reflect on or discuss to what extent information they are given can be generalized. Do you think the ancient Greeks always thought fluidly about what they considered an 'animal' or 'human' (or 'god')? Do you think all ancient Greeks felt the sphinx represented women as monstrous? Contextualizing knowledge can do much to move pupils from superficial to deep learning.

3.2.4 Step 4: knowledge co-creation

As a teacher, you might wonder whether your subject knowledge is extensive enough to broaden the scope of antiquity and deepen learning. However, in facilitating transformative learning, it is important to relinquish control over 'knowledge' as a teacher, at least to some extent. Naturally you know more than the pupils do about the cultures of antiquity, and you may have an elementary or more advanced knowledge of Latin and/or ancient Greek language. However, you do not need to know everything, even linguistically. Indeed, if you are a teacher who does not have much prior knowledge of Latin or ancient Greek, discovering the language alongside your pupils means you can compare notes on the metacognitive process. If pupils ask questions to which you do not have the answer, this in itself might be taken as a learning opportunity, in the form of homework for the pupils to look up for the next session or explore in assessment (see below). In this way, you 'co-create' knowledge together with your pupils, which means they take an active role in deciding what is considered 'knowledge'. Knowledge co-creation does not merely equate to unfocused group work. What it also does not entail is that you give up your authority as a teacher; quite the contrary.[32] What it means is that you as a teacher are aware of your personal views on antiquity and encourage your pupils to complement your view with their voices, under your guidance. Letting pupils add knowledge from their cultural and linguistic backgrounds is one easy way to co-create knowledge. It can be a slightly scary experience to allow pupils to discuss languages or cultures in class which you do not know. How can you be sure that the information they share is correct? In this context, it can help not to focus on individual pupils' contributions but on the knowledge that the group has assembled, asking about parallels and differences between answers with regard to language and culture. My students are trained to engage with pupils' home languages in each lesson in order to create a kind of collaborative linguistic knowledge bank in the classroom, in which the teacher plays a facilitating role rather than the only authority. Whenever new vocabulary or grammar is encountered, pupils are invited to discuss the concepts from their own linguistic repertoire, to which others can then respond. In this way, knowledge about language and identity is co-created through pupil participation.

In short, knowledge co-creation can take place at any level of the course: you can invite pupils to decide on the theme of the course or a lesson, or contribute to shaping activities or assessment. You might decide on a central theme of which they then explore parts – this plurality of voices can then arrive at a nuanced view of certain themes of antiquity. However, a great place for knowledge co-creation is in fact assessment, which is the next step.

3.2.5 Step 5: applied assessment

For the *Young Heroes* project, we work with non-linear language learning. This may sound like a contradiction in terms, but it means new linguistic knowledge is added very slowly and inductively, firmly integrated into a lesson's cultural content and with recurring consolidation of linguistic knowledge seen in previous lessons. In practice, not much linguistic knowledge is built up over our ten-hour courses: it takes pupils a few lessons to get to grips with the alphabet, so little grammar is taught (see the next chapter). Our focus lies on consolidation by means of repetition. The course is therefore not assessment driven: there is no fixed amount of Greek grammar or vocabulary pupils must acquire. Instead, they are allowed to keep their handouts with the alphabet and grammar with them at all times, so they can progress through the language at their own pace. However, we do in fact assess continuously, by letting pupils take part in quizzes, board games, and other games.[33] By dividing pupils into groups of various sizes, no pressure ever falls on one pupil alone, and information can be gathered from different pupils to get to the right answer.

We are in the luxurious position of not having to assess pupils formally but I want to offer some ideas for teachers wanting to develop assessment in line with the educational equity objective. To facilitate transformative learning, significant thought should go into whether or not to assess in the traditional way. As Jesse Stommel (2018) argues, '[t]he work of grading [tends to be] framed less in terms of giving feedback or encouraging learning and more as a way of ranking students against one another. Nods to "fairness" are too often made for the sake of defensibility rather than equity'. There are therefore basic questions you might want to check when setting any assessment from an equity perspective. Do you use language that you have explained in class, and keep instructions clear and specific? Do you clarify precisely which and how much information you expect? Do you offer different types of questions?[34] Considering these questions can go a long way towards allowing all pupils to do well on assessment. It is also useful to reflect on the number of marks you allocate to each exercise. If you ask a pupil to transliterate four ancient Greek words, it is important you score fairly. Asking for four equal pieces of information and scoring them out of three points makes marking more difficult, as the tendency will be to subtract what pupils get wrong, which leads to lower marks. Scoring for equity means scoring equally, based on all the information that is asked: each piece of the information puzzle would be reflected in the score in a constructive way, not just in grammar questions but across the board in tests and exams. Instead of subtracting what pupils get wrong, the correct information is added up and scored as a percentage (if a pupil gets 2/3 of an answer right, they should also get 2/3 of the points). By evaluating tests and exams in this way, many pupils achieve higher scores, not because standards have been lowered but because they are assessed constructively instead of punitively. Providing feed-*forward* instead of feed-*back* on assignments is also a useful tool. This means the teacher's comments are not (merely) critiquing the mistakes pupils have made but offer solutions for future assignments. Pupils may be encouraged to keep a list of this feed-forward with them to check at every test or assignment. This allows a teacher to have an immediate positive impact on transformative learning via assessment.[35]

However, knowledge of grammar, translation, and culture does not necessarily have to be assessed through tests, homework, presentations, or exams. The extent to which pupils have understood a certain block of information can also be assessed by letting pupils produce instead of reproduce content, in other words by letting pupils apply rather than repeat the information. Setting board games, blog posts, reflection reports, short stories, podcasts, or other creative activities as assessment can be extremely rewarding for a majority of pupils (though there are pupils who prefer productive assessment, and this is the reason why it is important to assess broadly). But how do you approach this in the context of multidiversity learning? How do you turn a 'creative assessment' such as taking part in a board game or writing a reflection text on an aspect of antiquity into a meaningful learning experience? How does a board game become more than a 'fun' activity?

What is important to understand about applied assessment is that it is not easier than standard assessments. Creating a board game, or writing a reflection text, might sound like 'fun' more than assessments which asks for direct grammatical, textual, or cultural information, but in order to do well, a pupil not only needs to have a firm grip on the content but also needs to be able to apply it to a specific context. This is tricky to do, yet a manageable (and desirable) difficulty,[36] since pupils are focused on the task rather than the grammar or linguistic element on which they are being assessed. Some of our school groups love Greek alphabet bingo, just about the most basic game invented. In a square divided into nine equal squares, pupils add nine random ancient Greek letters. The student-teacher then calls out random ancient Greek letters and pupils cross them off as letters are mentioned that are in their square. Whoever has a full square first shouts 'bingo'! While this is a playful way to consolidate pupils' knowledge of the alphabet, the applied nature of the exercise means pupils are focused on the game rather than the difficulty of certain letters which they have only just learned. Likewise, an exercise asking pupils to write a short text describing a day in the life of a particular ancient Greek person they have chosen invites them to write in Dutch while integrating ancient Greek words which they feel comfortable using (see Figure 3.3).[37] Such exercises can offer an appropriate challenge for each pupil, thereby offering automatic differentiation within a classroom. A board game my students created for the final lesson of the monsters course was really rather difficult, I felt, but the pupils loved it, as the group setting and playful format gripped them rather than the difficult grammatical and mythological questions they were asked to answer.

Assessment criteria might entail, for example, (1) understanding of the topic discussed, (2) clear links to the Latin or ancient Greek linguistic/textual/cultural aspect discussed, (3) critical application of (or engagement with) the information, and (4) development of a personal writing style. You might also mark communicative competence (how well a pupil communicates information) or intercultural competence, rather than – or alongside – grammatical correctness in Latin or ancient Greek, especially at an early stage. The use of such broad assessment criteria gives a broader picture of the knowledge a pupil has acquired than a strict focus on grammar, translation, and factual knowledge. Because pupils are applying knowledge, for them the focus is on the application and not on the learning itself, which makes the task more accessible. In an ideal curriculum, the use of such assessment would be developed throughout primary school, with reflection activities, for example, becoming increasingly complex each year. In this way, applied assessment can be a great tool to foster an inclusive learning environment.[38]

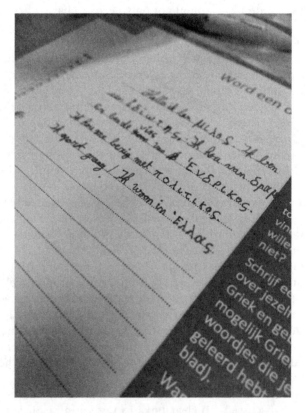

Figure 3.3 A pupil describes themselves as an ancient Greek child, using both Dutch and ancient Greek words.

3.2.6 Step 6: courageous conversations

There are, however, moments – such as the example I set out above – in any teacher's career in which their best intentions backfire, and conflict occurs in the classroom setting sparked by a learning activity. It is important not to freeze at such moments, and indeed anticipate that disorienting moments have the potential to lead to tension and, rarely, conflict. The SOAR-UP approach may help anticipate how to respond immediately when an incident occurs.[39] First, *Stop* before you respond: acknowledge that a discriminatory or hurtful incident has occurred, let the class catch their breath, and remember the only way to help is by not mirroring the perpetrator's anger or frustration. Secondly, *Observe* pupils' and your own reactions: are emotions running high; is the perpetrator angry, or the hurt party trying to shrug things off? Thirdly, *Assess* the situation: how explosive is it; how comfortable and competent do you feel in responding to the situation? Fourthly, *React*, not to the children but to their behaviour. Do you react directly or distract pupils instead, choosing to either delay your own reaction or – if you know you will be unable to resolve this personally – delegate the response, for example, to the head teacher? When you do react, *Use* active listening techniques and empathic communication focusing on pupils' experience of the incident. Finally, *Prepare* for potential future incidents by reflecting on what happened and how you might deal with it more appropriately.

However, how do you get primary school pupils so far as to want to enter into a courageous conversation with you?[40] This is no mean feat,[41] but I find Glenn Singleton's 2014 guidelines for 'courageous conversations' really useful when thinking about classroom engagement.[42] Singleton argues the following. First, 'stay engaged', so do not switch off or ignore the painful incident. Secondly, 'speak your truth', in a respectful and age-appropriate way. Thirdly, 'experience discomfort' and disorientation. This is key, as without holding this space of discomfort, no transformative learning is possible. And finally and most importantly, 'expect and accept non-closure', meaning it is not always possible to change pupils' attitudes, especially acquired attitudes of hostility towards entire social groups. It is possible to rework these guidelines as classroom directions, and apply them consistently so pupils may understand how courageous conversations may be shaped.

3.3 Conclusion: from disorienting dilemma to transformative learning

This final part of *SOAR-UP*, *Prepare*, brings me back to the start of this chapter: to those painful experiences pupils, my students, or I have faced in the classroom, and the reflection on transformative learning which this chapter has offered on the basis of my discussion of these disorienting experiences. It is important to acknowledge that tensions and conflicts arise because we each see the world through our uniquely tinted glasses, shaped as much by unconscious biases as by mindful insight. Often our worlds are compatible, sometimes they are not. During their school career, pupils tend to receive similar messages regarding their skills and worth in interactions with others, which either encourage or discourage them, as I discussed in Chapter 1. Throughout the years, our identity is shaped by this interaction with, and appraisal by, the outside world. We are shaped by the other, whether at home, in the playground, or at school, and tend to be slow to change our perspective once it is established. It is only when some experience strongly disrupts this perspective that transformation becomes possible and sometimes indeed inevitable. This is what the *Ancient Greeks – Young Heroes* project aims to do on the basis of the previous steps described in this chapter, namely disrupt the potentially damaging self-image pupils growing up in difficult circumstances have of themselves and offer them an opportunity to transform this image into a more constructive one through the study of ancient Greek.

For me, understanding this transformative potential of the work I was doing took more than ten years (and is still ongoing: sometimes it is impossible to anticipate where problems will arise). I learned the six steps described above through trial and error, as the examples in this chapter revealed. In the activity on shields and jewellery, I learned it is beneficial for pupils to contextualize activities for deeper learning (Step 3: '5Fs to 3Ps') and broaden our idea of antiquity so they would not, for example, associate shields necessarily with male soldiers (Step 2: 'Broadening the canon'). In my distressing god-drawing exercise, I learned about going back to the drawing board and sometimes scrapping an activity when it is not suitable for transformative learning aims (Step 1: 'Backward design'). Creating ancient curse tablets is an excellent assessment, on account of the object-based context in which to use certain ancient Greek grammar or linguistic knowledge (Step 5: 'Applied assessment'). In adapting the activity for pupils creating a monstrous self-portrait, pupils were invited to reframe the definition of the monstrous (Step 4: 'Knowledge co-creation'). Through the painful ethnicity-based incident, I learned a lot about the importance of conflict resolution in the classics classroom (Step 6: 'Courageous conversations'). I hope the steps I have set out above can help you not to fall into the same pitfalls as I have done over the years. Most of all, transformative learning starts from a teacher's willingness to see the limitations of their own world view, which is why teaching classics for social justice is not merely a transformative process for pupils but for teachers too.

3.4 Reflection tools

Some of the steps in this chapter may have been familiar to you, others are perhaps new. You will have felt, while reading, to which steps you resisted, which felt understood, and which sparked enthusiasm. To finish this chapter, I therefore once again turn to some tools for reflection, with the same answer key (Table 3.1):

- − − This is definitely not a priority for me.
- − I pay attention to this from time to time.
- − + I would like to pay more attention to this, but I'm not sure how.
- + I regularly pay attention to this.
- + + This is an integral part of my current thinking.

Table 3.1 Reflection tools

	− −	−	− +	+	+ +
I am able to empathize with the diverse problems which pupils I teach/work with face on a daily basis. ('Multidiversity')					
I have insight into my own biases and prejudice towards others (including pupils), whether positive or negative. ('Unconscious bias')					
I acknowledge to what extent my (classics) lessons are inclusive at the level of gender, religion, and ethnicity, and where adaptations are possible. ('Multidiversity')					
I reflect on ways in which the multidiverse needs of my pupils might take centre stage in the curriculum. ('Backward design')					
I see where, in my existing didactic resources, I might broaden my view of antiquity to make it more inclusive. ('Broadening the canon')					
Looking at existing didactic resources, it is clear to me where I apply the 5F principle (Food, Fashion, Famous people, Festivals, Flags, Folk dance, Fairs) and where I might make space for the 3Ps (Practice, Product, Perspective). ('From 5Fs to 3Ps')					

(Continued)

Table 3.1 (Continued)

	− −	−	− +	+	+ +
I understand the concept of knowledge co-creation and reflect on where I might make room for pupils' voices in the content and assessment of my courses. ('Knowledge co-creation')					
I am able to determine the extent to which my current assessments are inclusive, and where I assess punitively instead of constructively. ('Applied assessment')					
I can see where I might add applied assessment to my curriculum to offer a challenge for each pupil at their own level. ('Applied assessment')					
I am capable of considering teaching for multidiversity as a process and accept non-closure and discomfort. ('Courageous conversations')					
I feel confident in approaching primary classroom conflict and discrimination constructively. ('SOAR-UP')					
I recognize the place of disorienting dilemmas in the primary school classics classroom and how they might contribute to genuine transformation for pupils and myself. ('Transformative learning')					

Notes

1 Sierens 2007: 6 (my translation). I do not focus specifically on learning difficulties in our courses as differentiation is done on the basis of pupils' multidiverse needs, which include learning difficulties (among what Sierens calls 'mental faculties'). Hubbard 2003, Chanock 2006, and Hill 2006 explore useful case studies at secondary school level, while Susan Deacy's work on autism and classical myth is a wonderful case study at primary school level (https://myth-autism.blogspot.com/).
2 UNDP & Oxford Poverty and Human Development Initiative 2020: 25.
3 Crenshaw 1989.

4 Sierens 2007: 6, Valcke 2014: 279–397.
5 Greenwald & Krieger 2006.
6 Kahneman's 2011 *System 2* and *System 1* of the brain respectively.
7 Chapter 1, pp. 16–17 and Chapter 2.
8 D'Mello & Graesser 2014: 299.
9 Randolph & Johnson 2017. Mezirow 1991 argues that children do not have transformative learning, because their learning is merely formative, by means of authority figures. I disagree: while transformative learning by primary school children may take place at a more intuitive and subconscious level, it is possible to go beyond mere reflection to approach transformation. In spite of this and other criticism of Mezirow's terminology, it is nevertheless useful to think about the process involved in working towards transformative learning.
10 Karpiak 2006: 88.
11 Brookfield 2012: 72.
12 Gagarin 2010 c.f. 'jewelry'; MacDonald 2018 for women warriors.
13 We only discuss first- and second-declension nouns in that particular exercise, though pupils also come across other declensions. (Latin has five different morphological groups which all have different endings for different grammatical functions in the sentence; these are called declensions. The nominative case is predominantly used for the subject and predicate parts of the sentence.)
14 Gager 1992.
15 Bracke 2010.
16 Hannan et al. 2013.
17 The title is adapted from Ennser-Kananen 2016.
18 See this lesson: https://www.oudegriekenjongehelden.ugent.be/en/teaching-materials/course-1-monsters-in-storytelling-traditions/lesson-4-medusa/.
19 See p. 30.
20 Penrose 2014 and Strolonga 2014 describe similar classroom experiences regarding sexuality and religion respectively; Hunt 2022: Chapter 6 outlines further examples.
21 Freire 2005 [1970]: 48.
22 What follows develops some of the steps described in Bracke 2017 and 2021.
23 Wiggins & McTighe 2005, 2nd edition.
24 For further tools for diversity teaching, see Wagner, Perugini & Byram 2017.
25 https://onderwijsdoelen.be/.
26 See https://www.weekvandeklassieken.nl/#/Educatie for learning resources.
27 Bond 2019, Sawyer 2016.
28 See pp. 10-11.
29 RMO catalogue numbers F 1959/8.2 and GN-C_0730. See https://www.weekvandeklassieken.nl/#/Educatie lesson 2.
30 A huge debate on classics and whiteness underlies this argument. Dhindsa 2020 provides an introductory discussion.
31 Glynn et al. 2018.
32 Walsh 2016.
33 Godwin-Jones 2014; Faya Cerqueiro & Chao Castro 2015.

34 Adapted from Centre for Language and Education Leuven: http://www.taalbeleid.org/assets/downloads/lo_instrumenten_evaluatie_so_checklist_beoordeel_je_examen.pdf.
35 Hirsch 2017.
36 See p. 110.
37 https://www.oudegriekenjongehelden.ugent.be/lesmaterialen/cursus-1-identiteit/les-5/.
38 Many pupils in a multidiverse context are also multilingual. On the implications for assessment, see De Backer et al. 2020.
39 Center for Faculty Excellence 2004: 3–4.
40 Though focused on secondary and tertiary education respectively, Hunt 2016 and Rabinowitz & McHardy 2014 offer useful insights which can be applied to difficult conversations in the primary school classics classroom.
41 Taylor 2021, Ford & Maxwell 2013, Gross Davis 2009, 2nd edition: 57–71.
42 His focus is race, but this can be applied to other social axes.

4 Six 'how-to' questions on teaching Latin and ancient Greek language at primary school

4.1 Transformative curriculum-building in action

The steps I set out in the previous chapter should provide a solid starting point when designing a primary school classics curriculum which seeks to develop transformative learning. However, the practical application of these steps may still seem rather vague, or the actual process of putting them into practice daunting. For that reason, this chapter addresses the most basic practical questions regarding Latin and ancient Greek teaching at primary school: how do you start the designing process, teach the alphabet and grammar, approach texts, integrate pupils' language repertoires, and build up their vocabulary knowledge without rote learning? I will use the case study of the 'Monsters in storytelling traditions' course – one of the recent courses we created in the *Young Heroes* project – as a starting point for the exploration of these questions. It is a standard course in the *Young Heroes* curriculum which my students have now taught twice, in 2021 and (with some adaptations) 2022. It contains five lessons of 1h40mins to two hours each, which were taught weekly from the end of February to the end of March/early April. I will discuss each lesson as a case study to answer each question. At the end of this chapter, I will demonstrate how the responses to the various questions may be mapped onto a 'translanguaging' approach to teaching, which I defined in Chapter 1 as a current Modern Foreign Language approach which moves away from strict L1-to-L2 learning to focus on developing pupils' entire linguistic repertoire.

4.1.1 Question 1: how to design a transformative learning course?

4.1.1.1 Case study: the 'Monsters in storytelling traditions' course

The *Young Heroes* project aims to function as a disruptor of the downward spiral of decreasing aspirations experienced particularly by

DOI: 10.4324/9781003229742-4

children growing up in difficult circumstances,[1] by demonstrating to both pupils and teachers that they are able to deal with cognitively challenging subject matter (widening participation, Chapters 1 and 2), as the pedagogy has been adapted to integrate pupils' voices (transformative learning, Chapter 3). By changing stereotypical views of and by children growing up in difficult circumstances – their abilities and aspirations – the project is starting to function as a catalyst for social change. But whenever pupils are asked if they do linguistic exercises in ancient Greek lessons, most say they do not: they will talk about creating pots in clay, playing board games, or taking part in games in the playground. This is a deliberate pedagogic strategy: in order to make the ancient Greek language and grammar accessible, our student-teachers integrate language learning into interactive exercises, games, and artistic activities. I want to avoid pupils getting stressed about learning a difficult language; this can be achieved when they are busy enjoying the various exercises and therefore do not worry (much) about making mistakes. However, this does not mean we are teaching Latin or ancient Greek in a mere 'fun' way: in our courses, grammar and literacy are functionally embedded into every – appropriately challenging – activity rather than merely alternating reading or grammatical exercises with 'fun' activities.

It is not easy to frame engaging learning activities so that grammar and metalinguistic awareness are developed gradually throughout the course and individual lessons, while seeming challenging but 'fun' for pupils. When my students and I have our curriculum development meeting at the beginning of each school year, we do not start by talking about which myths or creative activities we want to teach the children. We rather follow a number of steps in a simple framework to help us set out the curriculum, after which we go on to create each individual lesson. This is a general framework I use for each course my students and I design. While it functions as a way to record work-in-progress, and the content is rearranged and adapted as my students go on to teach the actual classes, it is a good idea to start with such a general framework in order to clarify the general learning outcomes as well as the progression of individual classes within the greater whole. This is what my framework looks like (Table 4.1):

I start each course by brainstorming an appropriate overarching theme for multidiversity with my students (Step 1: backward design),[2] taking into account their personal interests and expertise, and which knowledge they would like to share with pupils. I tend to hone their suggestions until I am satisfied we have a solid theme that is broad enough to allow for creative applications, yet focused enough to allow

Table 4.1 Course framework

Overarching theme:				
	Lesson 1	Lesson 2	Lesson 3	Lesson 4 ...
Theme for multidiversity				
Grammar/ literacy				
Didactic approaches				
Link to pupils' experience				

for meaningful and potentially transformative interactions. When we came up with the 'monsters' course (short for 'monsters in storytelling traditions'), all of the student-teachers had an interest in mythology and storytelling. On the basis of a discussion I had with my students suggesting that a focus on heroes – interesting as it may be – may corroborate a binary world view of us ('hero') and them (the external 'monster' that must be defeated),[3] we decided on monsters in storytelling. This focus provided us with ample opportunities to nuance us-versus-them narratives, by zooming in on the monsters' experiences in stories of different storytelling traditions. With regard to learning outcomes, we do not only work towards the Flemish government's 'social skills' learning objectives, such as 'admitting being in the wrong, listening to criticism and learning from it', and 'cooperating with others regardless of social background, gender, or ethnicity',[4] which overlap with our general outcome of 'courageous conversations' (Step 6). We also work towards pupils having a broad and dynamic understanding of monster-related myths in antiquity (Step 2: broadening the canon; Step 3: from 5Fs to 3Ps), and the ability to contribute to co-creating knowledge about language and myth (Step 4), for example, through their active involvement in completing applied activities (Step 5). It is on the basis of these broad learning outcomes that the specific language-related outcomes are then set, which is what I will discuss presently.

Historically and conceptually, in our 'monsters' course, we broaden antiquity by integrating ancient Greek stories about monsters and heroes into a broader narrative, from the Mesopotamian Gilgamesh epic to Flemish folktales (Step 2). The Cyclops, for example, is linked with giants from the *Arabian Nights* as well as the giants from

Flemish folklore which parade through most towns each year.[5] Odysseus is compared with Gilgamesh – a hero whose story was popular throughout the Near East for 2,000 years – and Sinbad, a possibly seventeenth-century addition to the *Arabian Nights*.[6]

Once the general theme has been established, we move to the grammar learning outcomes of the course. While my aim in teaching ancient Greek is to support transformative learning, ancient Greek language learning does take a central position in this objective, and so I first schematize which linguistic elements we intend to teach to pupils. As pupils first need to learn the alphabet, the grammatical focus of lessons 1 and 2 tends to be similar in each course. In our two-hour lessons, lesson 1 is usually taken up with learning the alphabet and writing pupils' own and neighbours' names in ancient Greek, with a nominative singular ending of the first or second declension. Lesson 2 consolidates this knowledge by exploring noun endings in the nominative and accusative singular.[7] The grammar taught in remaining lessons tends to vary more, but is necessarily restricted, since we offer only five lessons each year and no new grammar tends to be introduced in the final lesson. Lessons 3 and 4 might teach, for example, first- and second-declension adjectives, the present active imperative singular and plural of verbs, or the present tense conjugation of εἰμι (*eimi*, 'I am'). We tend to make a rough decision in our first meeting, but details do still shift once individual classes are designed, usually because certain topics lend themselves better to a discussion of specific linguistic aspects. A class on movement, for example, whether in a mythological story or battle re-enactment, lends itself well to an exploration of the imperative, while describing mythological animals ('I find the griffin ... beautiful, ugly, interesting, horrible, terrifying', etc.) fits well with a discussion of adjectives. So while we do provisionally set grammar first, we know a lesson is well designed when grammar and theme are effectively intertwined. After we have set a course theme and have provisionally decided which grammar to teach, we move on to the design of individual lessons.

Within the overarching theme, I give my university students some time to brainstorm potential topics for specific lessons. For the 'monsters' course, we decided on the Minotaur as a topic for lesson 1, Cerberus for lesson 2, Medusa for lesson 3, giants (in particular the Cyclops) for lesson 4, and 'a hero's journey' for the final lesson. These may seem like obvious and perhaps 'simple' themes, but for each lesson, we hold true to our intention regarding the transformative learning potential the lesson should hold for pupils. We do this by integrating theme and grammar to work towards that objective.

Timing	Teaching Content	Didactic method/activity	Link to Flemish region curriculum Years 5 & 6	Organisation and developed material
35 mins.	Where and when did the ancient Greeks live?	Show a world map with all the continents. Discussion: in which continent is Greece located? (5 mins) Exercise in pairs (10 mins.) - What do pupils know or remember about continents? - What is their own background? - Where is Greece on the map? Where did the ancient Greeks live? (10 min.) Entire group: - Ask what the differences are between the 3 maps and why they are different. - Discuss that the borders of ancient Greece have changed significantly through time: Ancient Greece on 3 continents. Compare the maps with each other. - Explore causes for the changing borders When did the Ancient Greeks live? (10 min.) Group work for 2: - Pupils put the pictures in the correct chronological order on the handout by means of numbering - Full class discussion	OWru 6 Develop map comprehension, orientation and map skills. IKid1 Develop basic trust. TOtg3 Recognise the multilingual identity of fellow pupils and dare to use one's own multilingualism. SErv2 Experience the diversity of people as a wealth and make use of it. OWru4 Experience, explore, identify and express how people define spaces and use concepts of boundaries in the appropriate context. OWti5 Experience, explore and express how reality changes and knowledge about it evolves over time. OWti3 Explore and locate in time events from one's own life and from history.	Slides on PowerPoint with the world map, map of the ancient Greek empire, map of Alexander the Great's empire. Handout with images and timeline

Figure 4.1 Activity from the beginning of lesson 1 as formulated in a lesson plan.

Individual lesson plans are then structured to help student-teachers deliver their lessons effectively: each lesson plan documents timing, details about the practical learning activity, learning objectives addressed, and practical resources required, as exemplified in Figure 4.1.[8] We are not reinventing the wheel when it comes to lesson plan structure; indeed most schools' lesson plans are more complex than ours, but I do not want to have too much information clouding the overarching learning objectives. It is because of the way in which the content is approached that lessons are made accessible and potentially transformative, and this needs to be central in lesson plans.

4.1.1.2 Discussion

It is perfectly possible to teach an introductory course to Latin or ancient Greek – or indeed to classical cultures – covering general themes in each lesson, such as the gods, heroes, theatre, and daily life. I would indeed consider the first course my students taught at UGent, on the theme of 'identity', to be such a course.[9] However, by choosing a more specific theme not only based on your own interest and expertise but also relevant to children's own lived experience, as Step 1 ('backward design') in the previous chapter outlined, it is possible to delve deeper into a subject which addresses pupils' genuine needs, and therefore increase the potential for transformative learning. If you are teaching Latin or ancient Greek, consider also which basic grammar you would like to teach the children (if any), and to what extent you want to focus on etymology and vocabulary-building in particular lessons. All of this will also depend on your pupils: in our courses, each lesson plan is in fact altered slightly by each student-teacher to suit their particular class group. When designing lessons or an entire course, take into account that even a well-formulated framework will require adaptation along the way and revision in future years.

4.1.2 Question 2: how to teach the ancient Greek alphabet?

This is obviously only relevant for those teachers who want to teach ancient Greek, not Latin, yet it is a key question and I want to address it appropriately. There are various ways in which one might approach the Greek alphabet. Because my students teach the entire alphabet in the space of one lesson, I discuss the case study of lesson 1 of our monsters course as a starting point for further discussion.

4.1.2.1 Case study: the Minotaur – lesson 1 of the Monsters course

Each lesson of our courses is carefully planned, incorporating a limited number of complementary activities which all work towards the same outcomes. Lesson 1 is an introductory lesson in each of our courses. While it would be possible to start talking about the Minotaur immediately, I prefer pupils to understand what we mean by 'ancient Greek language', 'ancient Greece', and 'the ancient Greeks' at the start of our course. The first activities are therefore baseline activities, in order to establish, together with pupils, where and when the ancient Greeks lived. Simple as these exercises may seem, they have nevertheless changed a lot since I started teaching Latin in Welsh primary schools. As I outlined in Step 2 of the previous chapter ('Broadening the canon'), maps of Europe have been replaced by maps of the continents and Mediterranean, and a stationary map of 'ancient Greece' in the fifth century was replaced by two maps, one of the archaic period and another from the time of Alexander. The notion of changing borders helps pupils begin to understand the fluctuating concept of borders and identity, which is key in our courses. The question when the Greeks lived is explored in pairs, in a numbering exercise by means of which they put in chronological order living spaces and clothes throughout the ages. This exercise is a great tool to contextualize the ancient Greeks historically, since pupils will have heard about the ancient Egyptians and Middle Ages

You already know ancient Greek!

αὐτο

άτλας

βιος

ὀπτικος

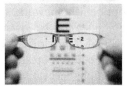

Figure 4.2 Pupils' first introduction to ancient Greek: 'You already know Greek.'

(or equivalent terms) too. Of course, the lesson material can only do so much: it is up to the teacher to engage in a discussion with pupils regarding relevant questions on geographical and chronological boundaries and their fluctuations.

Once contextualization is clear, we start by demonstrating to pupils that they already know some ancient Greek, in order to remove as many barriers to learning as possible before we start. My students show pupils a number of ancient Greek words on a PowerPoint slide with ancient Greek letters they already know or can easily read (see Figure 4.2). Using images as a scaffold, pupils are able to read and pronounce words such as αὐτο (*auto*), άτλας (*atlas*), βιος (*bios*), and ὀπτικος (*optikos*, 'visual' – the breathing/spiritus is only mentioned if pupils bring it up).[10] Starting with easily recognizable letters such as alpha (α), upsilon (υ), tau (τ), and omicron (ο), most pupils can in fact read eleven letters of the ancient Greek alphabet intuitively. It is only in the final word that the *pi* is introduced in classes which have already studied *pi* in a mathematical context. This exercise is trickier to prepare than one might expect: each year, I have discussions with students concerning words such as βιβλιον (*biblion*) or πλανητης (*planētēs*),[11] which I would argue are not appropriate at this moment, since the letters ν (*nu*) and η (*ēta*) are easily confused with the letters v and n, which might cause unnecessary stress. Note also that we consciously decided not to use accents, since I do not see a place for them in the context of our learning objectives: as our focus is on linguistic awareness, accents would only detract from that. That we never get to a point of confusion in the course because of a lack of accents validates this decision.

Learning the entire alphabet is a slow process on the interactive board. My students teach the entire lower-case alphabet at the board, while pupils trace letters and then re-write them with the help of handwriting lines on their handouts. Confusing letters such as *nu* (ν) and *ēta* (η) are highlighted at the appropriate moment. Pupils of all literacy abilities are able to trace the letters as many times as they wish. Capital letters are not normally taught in the course but provided to pupils as optional homework, though pupils who are really flying through the alphabet can be given this exercise in class if they are finished early. Alphabet bingo is used to consolidate pupils' understanding of the alphabet. Importantly, at all times pupils have their handout of the entire alphabet on the table with them, so they do not need to have memorized the entire alphabet in order to move forward in the course.

Student-teachers finally take pupils through a number of ancient Greek words with Dutch derivatives; this gives them an opportunity to sense pupils' grasp of the alphabet and intuitive understanding of the concept of derivation. By means of a discussion of these examples, the breathing and nominative singular endings are discussed inductively (see Figure 4.3). At this point, the student-teacher also points out other peculiarities, such as the spelling of kappa as c in Dutch, as

The alphabet of the Ancient Greeks			
Εὐρωπη	A α alfa	N ν nu	
σχολη	B β beta	Ξ ξ xi	
ἀτομος	Γ γ gamma	O o omikron	
βαρβαρος	Δ δ delta	Π π pi	
κυκλος	E ε epsilon	P ρ ro	
ὀργανον	Z ζ zeta	Σ σ sigma	
πολιτικον	H η eta	T τ tau	
ζωιον	Θ θ theta	Y υ upsilon	
	I ι iota	Φ φ fi	
	K κ kappa	X χ chi	
	Λ λ lambda	Ψ ψ psi	
	M μ mu	Ω ω omega	

Figure 4.3 A discussion of easily understood ancient Greek words encourages pupils to grasp the concept of derivation intuitively.

exemplified by κυκλος (*kuklos*, 'circle'), spelled *cyclus* in Dutch (*cycle* in English), and the tendency to drop the endings of derivations, as in the examples of σχολη (*scholē*, 'leisure') turning into *school*, ἀτομος (*atomos*, 'indivisible') into *atoom* (*atom* in English), and βαρβαρος (*barbarous*, 'non-Greek') into *barbaar* (*barbarian* in English).

Word endings and grammatical gender are then explored by means of words associated with the myth of the Minotaur: the names of the Minotaur (Μινωταυρος, *Minotauros*), Ariadne (Ἀριαδνη, *Ariadnē*), and *paidion* (παιδιον, 'child') are shown on a PowerPoint slide to aid a discussion on masculine, feminine, and neuter noun endings, to which children can contribute with information on the expression of grammatical gender in their own languages.[12] Student-teachers discuss with pupils the fact that often masculine or feminine gender and noun ending coincide, but there is a third ending for non-binary or in-between grammatical gender (see below). The inclusive construction of gender beyond the binary means each pupil is able to choose their own grammatical ending when they adapt their first name into ancient Greek.

Finally, through a discussion of the Minotaur myth, the concept of 'monsters' is introduced: what makes the Minotaur a monster (or not), and how might we define a monster? Can we generalize such a definition? To wrap up the lesson, pupils draw a monstrous self-portrait with their name in ancient Greek – with the ending of their choice – which they then share with the class in order to start the reflection on self and other, norm and monster.[13] This initial lesson hence teaches the alphabet on the premise that ancient Greek is already part of pupils' linguistic repertoire which can be expanded further, and starts the exploration of the concept of self and other.

4.1.2.2 Discussion

There are important decisions to be made when teaching the ancient Greek alphabet. Do you teach it deductively, as my example demonstrated, or inductively; over the course of one class or more; alphabetically or thematically, as letters pop up in names or activities? How do you let pupils practice writing the letters? Do you use accents or not, and how do you explain grammatical gender? A successful case can be made for each of these decisions, depending on the learning objectives of a specific course.

I tend to teach the alphabet deductively and alphabetically, in one class, since this means we can quickly start on our courses' social justice learning objectives. As pupils are allowed to keep their handout with the alphabet on their table at all times and my students spend time in each class on alphabet revision, most pupils are able to write all letters confidently by lesson 4. However, in the online course 'Fact and fiction' which I discussed in the previous chapter, we decided to teach the alphabet over the course of two online one-hour classes, and not alphabetically but as pupils came across the letters in the names of certain deities from the stories we discussed (Figure 4.4).[14] In this way, pupils learned how to spell the names Demeter,

δ

η

μ

η

τ

η

ρ

δημητηρ

Figure 4.4 Learning ancient Greek letters as part of words is one way for pupils to learn the alphabet in context.

Persephone, and Hades in lesson 1, and others in lesson 2, until they had practised all letters. Alternatively, you might, for example, use inscriptions to introduce ancient Greek letters in their specific context. There is indeed an advantage to teaching the letters in the context of words rather than as separate entities, though the learning process is perhaps slower and becomes a separate learning objective. I also feel there is something slightly unstructured about teaching the alphabet non-alphabetically, though that is perhaps the philologist in me resisting this approach. For younger pupils particularly, slow practice of, and play with, the alphabet might be useful – Therese Sellers' book *Alpha Is for Anthropos*, for example, offers songs and activities for each letter based on ancient Greek iconography, which will enthuse younger children. In short, how you teach the alphabet depends not only on the age group but also particularly on the learning objectives you want to address.

How pupils practice ancient Greek letters is entirely open to creative ideas, whether you get them to create clay pots or magical lead (i.e. aluminium) tablets, wax writing tablets or paper crowns, and indeed various activities can function as alphabet-writing practice in different classes. The two final questions – regarding accents and (though this anticipates the next question on teaching grammar) gender – are important to consider. First, unless pupils are being prepared for rigorous ancient Greek learning at secondary school, I do not see what accents might add to a primary ancient Greek course aimed at facilitating transformative learning, and I would therefore recommend excluding them. Secondly, regarding grammatical gender, making lessons gender-inclusive is unquestionably a challenge when you are teaching a language with grammatical masculine and feminine endings often corresponding with biological sex. In the courses I taught at Swansea, there were – as in *Young Heroes* – limited lessons in the project and the didactic focus was on more than just the language. Therefore, for the longest time, in lesson 1 when children were invited to write their name in Latin or Greek – be it on a crown, clay tablet, or wreath – my students taught only the masculine and feminine endings of the first and second declension, and explained these were for boys and girls respectively. It was only when I started to teach the course at Ghent that realized I had to bring more nuance to the binary distinction. Since ancient understanding of gender went beyond a binary distinction, and Aristotle's definition of the neuter as 'in-between' indeed allows for a non-binary interpretation,[15] I do not see why we should retain a binary simplification in an inclusive course. How you approach teaching this will again depend on the age group, but I would argue that, even if there are no pupils of non-binary gender in your specific class, it is still worth addressing the issue.[16] This will offer all children a means of identifying constructively in classics lessons.

4.1.3 Question 3: how to teach Latin or ancient Greek grammar?

Even though a Latin course does not require the teaching of a new alphabet, the first lesson of Latin courses I have designed over the years has always had a similar structure to the ancient Greek introductory lesson I outlined above: in order for pupils to understand the premise of what they are about to study, context is everything, and for that reason, I always start with who, when, where, and what (language) we are studying. After this contextualization, grammar can be introduced, yet as I have argued before, in our courses this is not done by means of reading texts nor by doing explicit grammatical exercises,[17] but by embedding the grammar into well-framed activities. In order to demonstrate our approach, I will again offer a case study – the second lesson of the Monsters course, on the topic of dog monsters – on the basis of which I will open up the discussion about the various ways in which one might teach Latin or ancient Greek grammar at primary school.

4.1.3.1 Case study: Cerberus – lesson 2 of the Monsters course

In lesson 2, Cerberus is the central figure in a discussion about dog monsters in various storytelling traditions, from the Egyptian god Anubis to the Japanese Okuri-Inu wolf spirits who follow people on mountain tracks, via werewolves in various traditions.[18] While the first lesson kept the alphabet and myth partly separate (so pupils received a strong foundation of their alphabet knowledge on which to build), from this lesson onwards, theme and language learning are strongly intertwined. By means of an interactive story delivered via PowerPoint presentation, pupils are invited to examine more deeply what defines a hero or monster, while also refreshing their knowledge of the ancient Greek alphabet and inductively learning about case endings. One of my students created a wonderfully interactive story in which the entire group of pupils can make decisions on each PowerPoint slide: do they want to play as a hero or as Cerberus, and which decisions do they want to make as they make their way through the underworld? Some decisions will lead to death and starting over, others will eventually lead to victory. Each slide is read aloud by one pupil, giving the teacher a chance to check individual pupils' grasp of the alphabet and reinforce difficult letters, after which the entire group raises either a green or orange card to make a decision. The majority decision is then acted upon, which leads to the next slide and the next decision. This Role-Playing Game is a popular lesson and pupils tend to want to take both roles of Cerberus and hero, and play out various scenarios.

As you can see in Figure 4.5, inductively the accusative ending is also introduced in this game: on this particular slide, 'κερβερος (*Kerberos*) is distracted' and pupils have a choice to either 'push κερβερον (*Kerberon*) aside' or 'sing a lullaby' to put him to sleep. Similar choices have to be made throughout the extended activity, which may seem simple but achieves a number of things simultaneously, namely (1) consolidating alphabet knowledge, (2) moving from letters to words and sentences integrating ancient Greek words into English or Dutch, and (3) introducing the accusative singular endings while at the same time (4) inviting pupils to think about heroic and monstrous decisions and identities. However, because pupils are focused on the decisions they are making within an essentially gamified classroom,[19] their focus is not on the complexities of the grammar. In the first slides of this activity, the change in noun endings is not brought up by the student-teacher. However, if pupils do not ask about it towards the end of the game, it is time to bring it up and ask pupils whether they have noticed anything in the spelling of the Greek words, and why they think the endings change. Grammatical terminology such as case names – the accusative in this lesson – are avoided deliberately in our courses. Instead, case endings are connected to grammatical terms used in pupils' school curriculum.

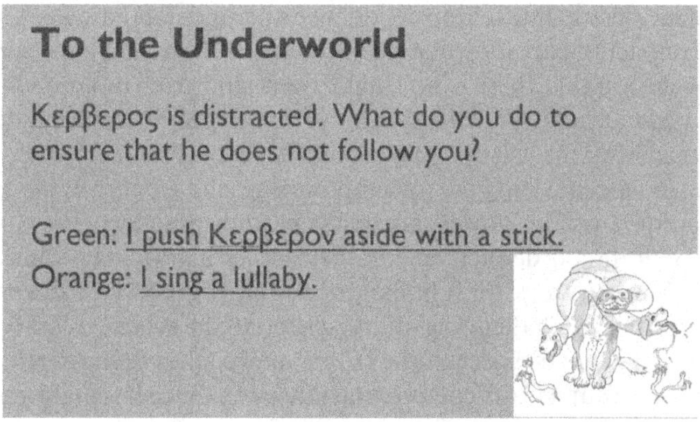

To the Underworld

Κερβερος is distracted. What do you do to ensure that he does not follow you?

Green: I push Κερβερον aside with a stick.
Orange: I sing a lullaby.

Figure 4.5 This co-creative game introduces the accusative ending inductively.

Pupils finally practice writing the ancient Greek alphabet while also further questioning what makes a 'monster', by doing a well-known exercise, namely folding an A4 paper in three, and then consecutively and secretly drawing the top, middle, or lower parts of a monster, while labelling the body parts in ancient Greek, using a list of words on the handout. Though this is an outwardly silly exercise which pupils know and enjoy, it becomes meaningful by framing it appropriately to further pupils' questioning of boundaries between the human and monstrous while practising spelling of Greek words and looking for connections within their linguistic repertoire.

4.1.3.2 Discussion

Do you teach grammar deductively or inductively; with a grammar-translation, reading-comprehension, living, mixed, or other didactic method?[20] Which 'point' in grammar do you want learners to reach? Which terminology do you use? These are difficult questions to which my answers have fluctuated over the years. I am personally a language learner who was happily educated on the basis of a rigorous grammar-translation approach. I remember, with a significant degree of embarrassment, being interviewed by Professor Keith Sidwell (one of the authors of the well-known secondary school *Reading Latin* course)[21] for a Latin teaching post at the Cork Summer School in Ireland roughly 20 years ago, and being shocked to find that grammar might be taught inductively, through reading a text.[22] I have since taught Latin and ancient Greek to pretty much every age group, from children as young as four years' old to adult learners, and over the years have reflected continually about how to teach grammar. When I collate my personal teaching experience and understanding of studies on the impact of classics teaching in the past 100 years, I have come to the conclusion that there is no single 'right' approach or course book, only a right approach for the specific group a specific teacher is teaching considering the learning objectives they have in mind.[23]

For the specific purpose of empowering children growing up in deprivation I would, however, exclude certain practices. First, while teaching grammar deductively on the basis of a grammar-translation approach might work for a homogeneous class group being prepared for linguistically challenging study at secondary school, research reveals that it is not as successful as other approaches in supporting pupils who grow up in difficult circumstances.[24] Teachers might instead use the reading approach, focus specifically on etymology, or indeed study Living Latin.[25] In all of these approaches, as well as ours which

I outlined above, pupils will learn grammar inductively. The differentiation between the various approaches is, indeed, a generalization, as most teachers will not use one approach exclusively. Whichever didactic approach you wish to take as your main one, it is important that you as teacher feel comfortable with it and with the didactic resources chosen or created, while acknowledging the need to differentiate in order to reach the entire class group.

Secondly, with regard to the amount of grammar pupils should learn or the 'point' they should reach on the scale to mastery, few or no official guidelines exist from national ministries of education. If you teach Latin for an entire year, you might reach the requirements for the UK-based OCR Entry Level Latin qualification, which stipulates as learning outcome knowledge of basic grammar and vocabulary, accurate translation of basic Latin sentences into English, understanding of unseen Latin, and understanding of derivations of English words.[26] This might be useful if you wish to prepare pupils for secondary Latin. However, for a transformative learning experience of either ancient language, an examination might actually be counter-productive, as I learned many years ago when a teacher and I decided to sign up a group of pupils – who had studied Latin for two years by then – for this examination. A number of pupils found the exam really stressful, even though we thought we had prepared them well. I decided never to put pupils through this again as part of our courses, though I did make them aware of this option in case they wanted to do the exam individually, which a few of them did in the following years. Any primary school classics course will nonetheless offer a reasonable amount of grammar for either Latin or Greek. This might include:

- verbs: the active present indicative, active present infinitive, forms of the verb 'to be', the active present imperative singular and plural
- nouns: at least the nominative and accusative endings, singular and plural of regular nouns of the first to third declensions (possibly also the dative and/or genitive)
- adjectives: first- and second-declension endings as well as the concept of agreement
- prepositions: the most well-known prepositions with the appropriate case, and applications in modern languages
- conjunctions: the use of conjunctions

These are certainly realistic goals if you aim to teach either Latin or ancient Greek for one hour a week for the duration of an entire school year, and the pupils who did Latin with me for two years indeed got further still.[27] However, 'further' is of course the key aspect of this issue, since one might ask to what extent more grammar means a better knowledge of Latin or Greek. In order to enable transformative learning, I would incorporate grammar into activities but let go of the notion of 'getting' to a strict point. Focusing on non-linear language learning would be more conducive to supporting pupils' development. My recommendation would therefore be to be ambitious, certainly – transformative learning does not mean no grammar ought to be taught at all or that 'anything goes': Latin and ancient Greek can indeed offer a 'desirable difficulty'[28] – but adapt your ambition as well as the learning outcomes to the needs of the specific target group you are addressing.

Finally, regarding grammatical terminology, I appreciate that there are colleagues who do use the standard grammatical terms – for example, for the cases or tenses – at primary school. If your aim is to prepare pupils for Latin or ancient Greek at secondary school, to introduce case terms so pupils may know them when they learn certain modern languages, or to support highly gifted pupils by offering them a linguistic challenge, this may indeed be the right approach for those specific contexts and learners. In a multidiverse classroom, where grammar is not the main learning outcome, I see no reason to include them. Just like ancient Greek accents or indeed vowel length symbols, I would argue that they only function as additional information which detracts from the main learning outcomes.

4.1.4   Question 4: how to integrate pupils' home languages?

This is not a standard part in every primary school classics course, but as I explained in Chapter 2, in our context it is. Incorporating pupils' home languages into the primary school classics classroom is not easy, as my story of the discrimination of a minority language speaker which I discussed in the previous chapter reveals. This is a rare case, however, and the benefits of integrating pupils' home languages in the classroom far outweigh the risks. Different home languages may not necessarily benefit pupils when they start learning ancient Greek, but the integration of different languages helps pupils learn about similarity and difference at a linguistic and cultural level. There are nevertheless varying degrees to which one might foreground this practice. While I feel I personally still have much to learn about this, I again offer a case study from our own course to exemplify how one might go about integrating home languages.

4.1.4.1 Case study: Medusa – lesson 3 of the Monsters course

Pupil feedback repeatedly shows that the third lesson in the Monsters course, about Medusa, is everyone's favourite: by now pupils have a fair grasp of the alphabet, can read many ancient Greek words, and have begun to understand our approach of questioning the monstrous. The myth of Medusa is ideal to further pupils' engagement. After a discussion of snake monsters in different cultures, the student-teacher reads aloud the story of Medusa adapted from Hesiod and Ovid,[29] while pupils are asked to listen actively to the story so they can fill in the names of characters in Medusa's family tree on the handout. This exercise introduces the vocabulary for the most popular activity in the entire course, in which pupils have to connect words for family relationships (father, mother, sister, brother, etc.) in five different languages (this is done intuitively, helped by colour-coding), add the respective words from their home language/s, and discuss the parallels and differences (see a filled-in example in Figure 4.6). This exercise takes up most of the lesson, as the different languages and their places on the Indo-European family tree are discussed, and the terminology is then applied to the Medusa story.

Familieleden

Oudgrieks	Nederlands	Frans	Engels	Duits	Eigen ta(a)l(en) Roemeens	Perzisch
μητηρ *meiteir*	moeder	mère	mother	Mutter		
πατηρ *pareir*	vader	père	father	Vater	maral	maudar
αδελφη	zus	soeur	sister	Schwester	tati	padar
αδελφος	broer	frère	brother	Bruder	sora	gwaur
θυγατηρ	dochter	fille	daughter	Tochter	frate	barandar
υιος	zoon	fils	son	Sohn	fică	dogtar
παιδια	kinderen	enfants	children	Kinder	ful	bacha
					copii	oeshtoekou

Figure 4.6 Pupils fill in their own languages next to the words for family relationships in European languages.

4.1.4.2 Discussion

As I mentioned in Chapter 2,[30] integrating pupils' home linguistic repertoires constructively in a classroom context is, in spite of the research which suggests its usefulness, still controversial practice, in the Flemish context at least. This is based on the age-old adage that, in Flanders, children should speak Dutch so they may integrate (more) fully. Even if teachers are open to a more inclusive approach, they might consider themselves lacking in competence when dealing with pupils' different home languages. For that reason, to what extent home languages are integrated into classics lessons depends on the teacher's – or the school's – language ideology. It is indeed perfectly possible to leave home languages outside of the primary school classics classroom entirely and only focus on Latin or ancient Greek, yet in order to enable transformative learning for pupils, it is in fact vital that their home cultures and languages are given a voice in the classroom. I feel I have much to learn about this yet, as I sometimes struggle to incorporate this approach into each and every lesson. Pupils, moreover, tend to get so excited sharing their stories that time management sometimes goes out of the window. However, I do feel there is much potential in this approach, particularly because of the clear enthusiasm this evokes in pupils year in and year out.

We do already bring home languages into the classroom in lessons other than the Medusa lesson. When discussing derivations, pupils are always asked if they know any languages other than Dutch – I am sure this is something many teachers do. It is, however, possible to take the approach further. In the first lesson, for example, my students ask pupils to fill in the 'language passport', created by the Ghent Education Centre, at the start of each course (Figure 4.7).[31] This requires a dialogue with individual members of pupils' family, in order to find out which languages they use (the form deliberately leaves out whether that means speaking, listening, reading, or writing, and to what level). Pupils tend to be keen to share their 'language passport', which demonstrates that bringing the project into the home environment is one way of making pupils feel safe enough to bring the home environment into the classroom.

My plan for the near future is to experiment further with incorporating home languages into the classics classroom. Since pupils are already used to the blending of Dutch and ancient Greek words in reading, writing, speaking, and listening activities, I will invite the incorporation of words from their home languages where they are

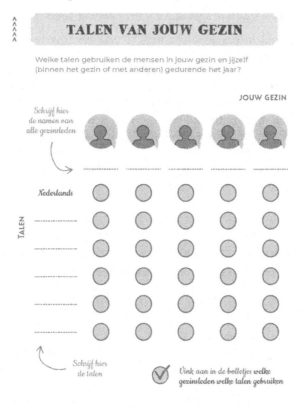

Figure 4.7 The Ghent Education Centre language passport is an accessible means of gauging pupils' language use.

unsure of the Dutch. This is not meant to be an easy way out for either pupil or teacher. On the one hand, it merely reflects what pupils are already doing when thinking about answers to certain exercises. On the other hand, by allowing them to use their full linguistic repertoire from all of the languages and linguistic registers they know, rather than avoiding certain phrases or sentences because they do not know a word, their full engagement with an activity will allow the teacher to see where support might help pupils expand their repertoire in either Dutch or ancient Greek further. Particularly for children who have only recently arrived in the Flemish region, this approach might ease their way into the Flemish educational system – more about this in the conclusion to this chapter.

4.1.5   *Question 5: how to approach Latin or ancient Greek texts?*

As I have said in previous chapters, I take reading texts – whether in Latin or ancient Greek – as a learning outcome rather than as a starting point, because of the challenge which reading chunks of text pose for the majority of the pupils we work with. When teaching 10- to 12-year-olds in our target group, I find that they tend to be ready to start reading short Latin or ancient Greek texts towards the middle of the second term of tuition – this is of course not something we reach in the current format at Ghent University, which is unfortunate. A discussion of the Cyclops lesson from the Monsters course will provide a starting point for further discussion about approaching texts.

4.1.5.1   *Case study: giants – lesson four in the Monsters course*

The Cyclops is the central figure in this course, but because not all giants from other storytelling traditions are one-eyed, we wanted to keep the theme broad enough to incorporate them. In fact, Flanders has a strong giants tradition, with wooden giant figures being carried through towns during annual festivals.[32] Connecting these figures with giants from the Gilgamesh and Sinbad stories as well as the Odyssean Cyclops highlights the diversity of such traditions throughout the world. After an initial discussion about the various giant traditions, pupils work towards understanding a Dutch-medium text about Odysseus and the Cyclops, which integrates a number of known and new ancient Greek words in the nominative and accusative singular (and in one particular school group, the plural). However, in spite of the engaging theme, this is not – as we learned from pupil feedback – necessarily an easy lesson.

Pre-reading is a technique I learned from doing Modern Foreign Language training in the UK: in order to move slowly from word to sentence to text level, a text is introduced which pupils are not asked to understand, but first explore by means of active listening and speaking, reading and writing, to aid contextual understanding.[33] This approach aims to remove tension from being confronted with a text. The short text about the Cyclops was cut into pieces of one sentence each. Each group of pupils received a full cut-up text of which the sentences had been mixed up. First, pupils were asked to put up their hand holding the particular sentence/s they had been allocated when they heard them in the story as the student-teacher was telling it. Secondly, groups were asked to put their cut-up story in the correct order while they listened to the story again. Next, pupils were asked to come to the front of the class and read out one sentence from the story in their best giant voice. A number of gapping exercises next invited pupils to come to grips with the actual words in the text and start understanding what it is about. Only then was the meaning of the text discussed in the whole class through comprehension questions and some translation. While most pupils did enjoy this activity, it was not an unequivocally successful lesson. Some pupils found the pre-reading too repetitive, others too challenging, so my plan is to rework the lesson for the future by making the text itself more interesting and less repetitive, as I know from previous experience teaching straightforward Latin texts at Swansea University that the format has the potential to work well for transformative learning. The *Young Heroes* project is a work-in-progress, and there are always elements that can be improved.

4.1.5.2 Discussion

The key difference between the reading approach and ours is that my students teach ancient Greek by gradually incorporating Greek words in Dutch sentences until pupils feel competent working with ancient Greek sentences and then texts. Pre-reading is one particular way to help pupils bridge levels, but there are of course others: pupils indeed create their own phrases, sentences, and then texts incorporating both ancient Greek and Dutch to the extent they feel comfortable in particular exercises, thereby gradually acquiring a more active knowledge of the target language. This may seem like an unusual approach,[34] but it can be highly effective, since it provides a linguistic background in which ancient Greek words can be contextualized and understood, thereby extending pupils' linguistic repertoire. This is demonstrated by the statistically significant increase in reading comprehension made by pupils taking part in our project in comparison with control groups of pupils who did not.[35]

I actually started using this approach when teaching Latin to four- to ten-year-olds many years ago during a summer school. In a first lesson, I added the translation of English words in Latin to the story of Romulus and Remus as I told it to pupils who were asked just to listen: 'This is a story (*fabula*) about a woman (*femina*) called Rhea.' The Latin words were repeated a number of times together with the children, and were repeated throughout the story, with my asking pupils: 'What is "story" again?' (They all respond: '*fabula*'!). In another lesson to the same age group, I introduced words for body parts by integrating them in English instructions for doing a sun salutation exercise in a yoga class. By increasingly integrating Latin words, we were in fact able to do an entire sun salutation in Latin by the end of the course.

This approach can be used to work towards the reading approach – as I intended when I first started using this approach when teaching 10- to 12-year-olds in the UK – or be integrated into it, for example, for differentiation purposes.

If you are unsure to what extent the pupils you have in mind would be supported by reading texts from the start or by working towards that level, how you might approach texts with your class, and to what extent your focus lies on listening or speaking, reading, writing, or translation, I would suggest you experiment to see what suits you and your pupils best. Indeed, I know a number of teachers in Britain who (at least used to) complement their reading-approach course book with our resources, so as I said, the divide between the different approaches is not as strict as it might appear.

4.1.6 Question 6: how to build up linguistic knowledge without rote learning?

4.1.6.1 Case study: the hero's journey – lesson 5 of the Monsters course

The final lesson of the Monsters course consists predominantly of a board game (Figure 4.8) which provides an informal setting for revision. Pupils play the game in groups of three and choose to play as Odysseus, Sinbad, or Gilgamesh trying to get home. Each pupil moves across the board horizontally or vertically by means of a pawn, which can move the number of steps that they throw with the dice in any direction. Pawns cannot move onto the square with rocks, are moved from one whirlwind to another when they land on one, have to take a 'chance' card when they land on a 'kans' ('chance') square and have to go to all four squares of their colour (light blue for Odysseus, green for Sinbad, and red for Gilgamesh) before they are allowed to go home. The first one home wins. Each coloured square they land on requires pupils to deal with a specific monster, or answer a myth question relating to content and/or grammar. Throughout the game, they will come across many parallels between the three myths and the monsters in them which will help them answer their questions. They will also have to answer questions about the linguistic elements of the myths they have discussed in the previous weeks, but they can help each other where possible. Pupil feedback tells us that pupils enjoy this story-based board game to end the course, and do not see it as assessment, even if it is a way to synthesize the content of the past five weeks and evaluate what pupils have

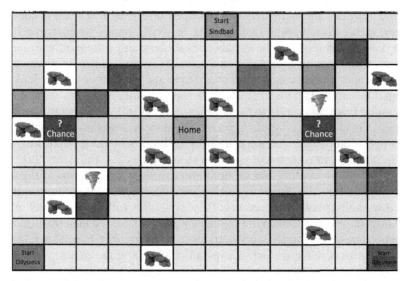

Figure 4.8 In this board game, pupils play as Odysseus, Gilgamesh, or Sinbad trying to get home.

gained from the course. Student-teachers go around helping each group so they can provide support where necessary.

4.1.6.2 Discussion

The approach in my project is clear: there is no rote learning of either vocabulary or grammar.[36] This is possible because our project is assessment-less. However, it can also be achieved within an assessment environment: in our courses, when school teachers decide that the exercises and homework my students give to pupils have to be marked, we make sure marks are given for 'communicative [... and] intercultural competence' where possible, rather than (or alongside) grammatical correctness.[37] As the case study exemplifies, there is not one way to expand pupils' linguistic repertoire, but we in fact do use a number of complementary strategies to encourage development of pupils' linguistic repertoire at their own pace. These have been discussed in my responses to the previous questions, but I gather them all here to give an overview. First, the course is non-linear, which means vocabulary and grammar are repeated in different exercises, though by means of different themes which keeps pupils engaged at their own level. This means pupils have ample opportunity to come into contact with vocabulary and grammar in different stories, contexts, and activities and ultimately store them by understanding them in context rather than through rote learning. Secondly, pupils are encouraged to keep the handouts of the alphabet, vocabulary, and grammar they have seen with them on their desk. This means they have control over which words and grammar they deem understood and which they want to look up. On handouts with linguistic exercises, a summary of the required grammar is always given to facilitate learning. Thirdly, by integrating ancient Greek or Latin words into Dutch sentences as well as working on progression towards full ancient Greek or Latin sentences, pupils learn the language in a known linguistic context, which decreases stress about correct understanding and pronunciation so they can progress at their own pace. Fourthly, by incorporating home languages into the course and encouraging pupils' connection of those languages with ancient Greek or Latin, more opportunities are created for pupils to expand their linguistic repertoire on the linguistic connections they feel comfortable making. Finally, most of our lesson activities entail small or large group work, which means pupils are able to support each other in their learning process.

Ultimately, my answers to these questions depend on a question already raised in Chapter 2,[38] namely what we actually mean by 'ancient Greek' or 'Latin' teaching at primary school. Is it taking part in 'fun' activities, being able to read short texts, speak the language at a basic level, and/or understand basic grammar? To end this chapter, I want to return to this issue and address it on the basis of the answers I have given to the previous questions.

4.2 Conclusion: transformative learning through a translanguaging approach

The answers to the questions I have tried to formulate in this chapter – about which 'point' of a language primary school pupils should reach in a course, to what extent more grammar means a better understanding of the language, how pupils might usefully integrate their home languages to learn the target language, and to what extent reading, writing, speaking, listening, or translating should be highlighted – all boil down to one thing, namely to what we as teachers think it means to 'learn' Latin or ancient Greek, specifically at primary school; to what counts as 'knowing' a language. All of these questions, and the different responses to them which I have explored, are never neutral but indeed inherently tied up in 'language ideologies', which I discussed in Chapter 1.[39] When we as teachers make decisions on the way in which we want to approach teaching a new language to our pupils, we do so within an ideological framework. When we consider that there is a 'point' which pupils should reach in order to 'have' ancient Greek or Latin; that 'only' Dutch and/or Latin/ancient Greek should be used in class; that a particular didactic method (e.g. rote learning) with its associated assessment is required for linguistic attainment, we are working in what is called monolingual language ideologies. These substantiate 'the role of separate, bounded languages with close links to nationality and ethnicity [… and] are responsible for concepts such as the native speaker norm and the target language immersion classroom upheld as key tenets of language learning today'.[40] The 'native speaker norm' means there is an 'ideal' native speaker whose linguistic usage a learner should approximate in order to be considered fluent, while the 'immersion' classroom practice holds that the use of other languages in the classroom environment will interfere in the learning process of the target language, as linguistic knowledge should be transferred directly from L1 (the main classroom language) to L2 (the new language). It is in this context that we can understand Flemish politicians' worry about home languages being spoken in the classroom, and their emphasis on the need to practice Dutch as much as possible. However, this premise does not correspond to historical reality, since few countries or communities have ever been truly monolingual, and language learners constantly apply their entire existing repertoires outside of the classroom context without thinking about it. Moreover, the notion of the 'native speaker' end goal for language learning tends to be biased towards a standard variety of language spoken by the educated class in power, marginalizing and disempowering speakers of non-standard registers.[41] Classics is – as I discussed in Chapter 1 – often seen as a key symbolic component of this particular language ideology.

But this also means that adopting a different definition of what it means to 'know' classics can lead to Latin and ancient Greek teaching taking on an empowering and transformative function. A different view of language learning indeed emerges when we shift from looking at languages as entirely separate codes, to the unique 'linguistic repertoire' (a term I have already used in this chapter, but which I will elaborate on now) of individuals which can be deployed to support learners in expanding it. This is the practice of 'translanguaging', meaning 'the deployment of a speaker's full linguistic repertoire without regard for watchful adherence to the socially and politically defined boundaries of named (and usually national and state) languages'.[42] Translanguaging is not about pupils just switching codes (from Dutch to ancient Greek to French, for example) but about them using their entire existing linguistic repertoire – including any languages they already know, to whichever extent they know them, as well as any linguistic registers (dialects, slang, jargon) of those languages

– in order to then expand it. It does not mean 'anything goes', but, on the contrary, encourages pupils to be brave in using their full linguistic repertoire rather than only what they believe is allowed within this specific classroom context, which might cause them to remain silent, hesitate, feel ashamed or embarrassed, and progress slowly if at all. Using a translanguaging approach does not entail that the use of any languages is permitted in any assessment, but that the entire linguistic repertoire can rather be activated in the learning process. It is also not a scaffold to monolingualism: it is rather a shift in learning objectives, from reaching a 'native speaker' level to being able to communicate meaningfully with the support of one's full linguistic repertoire. Importantly, this meaningful communication is achieved through the social practice of language: as the entire class group engages in translanguaging, this learning allows for non-dominant knowledge and practices to become visible within the classroom environment, thereby enabling pupils to reach a more nuanced view of themselves and the world around them.[43]

While it holds a symbolic place in monolingual language ideology, classics can therefore also be taught from a translanguaging approach. Conceptually this is done by shifting what it means to 'know' or 'have' either language, away from the 'end' result of 'having' certain grammar or being able to read certain texts.[44] Instead, a meaningful expansion of pupils' linguistic repertoire is aimed at through a learning process in which their entire current repertoire – not just in the classroom language and target language – is activated. I did not want to start this chapter by stating I would explain how one might go about teaching classics from a translanguaging approach. For it was not until a few years ago that I realized this is what I had been doing from the start, both as an act of resistance to what I perceived as an altogether narrow definition of 'classics', 'Latin', and 'ancient Greek', and as an attempt to disrupt the educational function of classics of differentiating between those who 'have' it and those who are, on account of their lack, considered as somehow deficient. I therefore wanted to take you, the reader, through the practical applications which I have explored, practised, failed, and refined them throughout the years. Teaching classics to entire class groups while working on internal differentiation has indeed proved possible by removing a specific 'point' pupils have to reach in a non-linear course (Question 1) while foregrounding meaningful communication about identity and the role of language therein. Learning the ancient Greek alphabet [Question 2] and grammar playfully (Question 3) can thereby be framed so it becomes a tool to enable this meaningful communication. Activating pupils' full linguistic repertoire through exercises integrating Dutch and ancient Greek/

Latin (Question 4) allows pupils to expand this repertoire more easily. Constructively integrating pupils' home language/s into the classroom environment (Question 5) adds to a classroom practice which recognizes and values every pupil's unique linguistic resources. Finally, by facilitating group learning of ancient Greek or Latin (Question 6), an incredibly rich linguistic social practice becomes visible in the classroom, giving a voice to hitherto silent aspects of children's identity.

Of course, any language lesson – taught from whichever language ideology – has the potential to be transformative for specific pupils. But in order for us to work towards a world with social justice in which misconceptions and stereotypes of others are challenged and disrupted, it is pivotal that we enable pupils from an early age to start reflecting on cultural biases and stereotypes, thereby paving the way for potential adaptations (transformations?) to their social practices.[45] As pupil feedback on our courses has demonstrated, the didactic approach we take – which is grounded in translanguaging principles, resisting a monolingual language ideology – enhances the potential for meaningful communication and transformative learning.

4.3 Reflection tools

To finish this chapter, I once again turn to some tools for reflection. If you have been thinking about designing a course for pupils in your area, you might use this framework to start thinking about what to teach. Are the priorities listed on the left yours too, or would you add different ones?

In order to help you fill in this framework, the following open reflection questions, in the order in which they were explored in this chapter, might help. I would invite you to reflect on your own thoughts regarding transformative primary school classics, whether in your current practice or plans for the future (Table 4.2).

Overarching theme:

	Lesson 1	Lesson 2	Lesson 3	Lesson 4	...
Theme for inclusivity					
Grammar/literacy					
Link to pupils' lived experience					
Didactic methods					

Notes

1 See p. 6.
2 See pp. 45-47.

Table 4.2 Questions for reflection

1 Which theme/s relating to antiquity do you think would be useful at primary school level, based on your own interests and expertise? What knowledge would you like to share with particular school groups?

2 [Ancient Greek only: How do you plan to teach the ancient Greek alphabet?]
 	
  a In one lesson or more
  b Deductively or inductively
  c Alphabetically or thematically

3 What are your current thoughts on how to teach the grammatical gender?

4 How will you teach Latin or ancient Greek grammar?
 	
  a Inductively, deductively, or a combination of both?
  b With the grammar-translation, reading, or living approach, or mixed?
  c Using grammatical terminology or not?

5 Have you got a course book or existing resources in mind, and how do these fit in with your preferred teaching approach?

6 Which Latin or ancient Greek grammar would you like pupils to learn?
 	
  a [Ancient Greek only: knowledge of the alphabet]
  b Nominative and accusative singular of first, second (and third) declension nouns and adjectives
  c Active indicative present of regular verbs
  d Active imperative/infinitive present of regular verbs
  e Basic forms of the verb 'to be'
  f ...

7 To what extent do you feel confident about integrating home languages into the classics classroom?
8 How do you currently think you would approach the reading of texts? As starting point or learning outcome? To what extent does the focus lie on listening, speaking, reading, writing, or translating?
9 Where do you stand on rote learning in ancient Greek or Latin lessons at primary school?
10 What are your current thoughts on teaching classics within a translanguaging didactic approach?

3 That is just one interpretation. It would also be possible to offer a nuanced, inclusive approach to heroes themselves – perhaps another year.
4 See p. 55.
5 https://www.oudegriekenjongehelden.ugent.be/en/teaching-materials/course-1-monsters-in-storytelling-traditions/lesson-3-giants/.
6 For more information on the links between these narratives, Dalley 1991, Louden 2011.
7 For the nominative, see Chapter 3 n. 13. (The accusative is – among others – used for the direct object.)
8 The curriculum mentioned in column 3 is the Flemish educational curriculum for 10- to 12-year-olds.
9 See https://www.oudegriekenjongehelden.ugent.be/lesmaterialen/cursus-1-identiteit/.
10 *Auto* ('self', hence an *auto-mobile* 'moves by itself'), *atlas* (the name of the Titan god holding up the sky in Greek myth), *bios* ('life', hence a *bio-scope* in Dutch means viewers are 'looking at life'), and *optikos* ('visual', with derivatives such as optician). The spiritus is a mark on top of vowels and the letter rho which indicates aspiration ('h') or not at the beginning of a word.
11 *Biblion:* 'book'; *planētēs:* 'wanderer' used for planets.
12 Dutch has the same three genders as ancient Greek, though masculine and feminine are largely invisible in daily language. Most children will already have studied French and will therefore be familiar with three genders. However, discourse in relation to home languages other than Dutch and French usually adds nuance to this discussion.
13 See pp. 55-56.
14 See https://www.weekvandeklassieken.nl/#/Educatie.
15 Aristotle *Poetics* 21. Hendrickson 2020 offers a great discussion about grammatical gender; Libatique 2020 discusses inclusive grammar use in general.
16 This Cambridge University Press poster on inclusivity in our Latin classroom offers interesting adaptations to make Latin texts more inclusive: https://issuu.com/cupeducation/docs/inclusivity_latinclassroom.
17 Hunt 2022: Chapter 1.
18 Okuri-Inu: Knight 1997; werewolves: Ogden 2021.
19 Godwin-Jones 2014.
20 See pp. 36-38.
21 Jones & Sidwell 2016, 2nd edition.
22 Needless to say, I did not get the job. A few years and a lot of teaching experience later, however, I did teach at UCC during the Summer School using the reading approach, and had a wonderful time.
23 Indeed, as Robson and Lloyd (*forthcoming*) argue with regard to beginners' Latin courses at university level, not one particular factor – the course book, length of the course, or didactic approach – was a determinant of student success, but rather a complex 'series of interactions between the teacher (and their preferred pedagogical approach) and the student (and *their* preferred learning approach) with the textbook and class dynamic [...] forming a crucial part of the mix'.
24 This does not mean that grammar is not discussed; on the contrary: it is a focus on grammar which can support pupils who struggle with literacy. See also Bracke & Bradshaw 2020.

25 See pp. 36-38.
26 See https://www.ocr.org.uk/Images/313158-specification-entry-level-latin-r447.pdf. The vocabulary list on pp. 23–27 of this specification is useful for beginners' Latin learning. The Greek specification no longer exists, though there are apparently plans to revive it.
27 For example, to the active indicative imperfect and perfect, and pronouns and adverbs.
28 D'Mello & Graesser 2014: 306.
29 Hes. *Theog.* 274-81; Ovid *Met.* 4.604-5.263.
30 See p. 30.
31 See https://meertaligheid.be/content/4-onderzoek/talenpaspoort-gezin.pdf.
32 My town's (Dendermonde) giants are listed as intangible UNESCO heritage: https://ich.unesco.org/en/RL/processional-giants-and-dragons-in-belgium-and-france-00153.
33 See Hunt 2022 for a discussion of these four aspects of language learning.
34 It is also used by projects such as Aequora in the US; see Butterworth 2017.
35 See pp. 33-35.
36 On vocabulary acquisition, see Hunt 2022: Chapter 1.
37 Seltzer & Wassell 2022: 28. See pp. 61-64 on Applied Assessment.
38 See pp. 36-38.
39 Woolard 2020: 1.
40 Trentman & McGregor 2021: 1.
41 Burns 2018 for the example of Spanish as taught in the US.
42 Otheguy et al. 2015.
43 Seltzer & Wassell 2022: 31.
44 I appreciate reading complicated texts in the original language is not the aim of (m)any primary school classics course(s), yet if primary school classics is taught based on the underlying principle that there are specific skills you need to 'have' Latin or ancient Greek, this will impact on the didactic method and class content used even at primary school.
45 Nieto 2010; Glynn et al. 2014.

5 Community engagement between pupils and policy

5.1 Ripples of community engagement

As I said at the start of this book, when I started the *Literacy through Classics* programme at Swansea University in 2011, my aim was to combine employability (increasing professional skills of university students) with widening participation (increasing awareness of and access to classics among disenfranchised non-traditional target groups). I was excited by how the project might benefit around 60 pupils and ten students per year, but did not think beyond that.[1] However, throughout the years, not only did my thinking about the project develop far beyond mere employability and widening participation, to a focus on social justice as I have framed in the previous chapters. The impact of both *Literacy through Classics* and, when I moved to Belgium, *Ancient Greeks – Young Heroes*, also started to ripple beyond the classroom: sometimes in obvious ways, through teachers and parents, but often in surprising ways which I could have never foreseen. It may not be as significant an aspect as the actual classroom practice and I will therefore keep this chapter brief, but it is nevertheless important to go beyond merely widening participation in classics (Chapter 1) and adapting the pedagogy so all pupils are heard and seen (Chapters 2 and 3). We must also acknowledge that, just as pupils and teachers come into the classroom with their own backpack full of ideas they have picked up outside of it, offering social justice–focused classics at primary school is not only shaped by but also in its turn has impact upon society at large. In order to offer meaningful transformative learning potential to pupils, it is therefore vital to embed their learning in the communities in which they grow up. The following reflections on my own practice – and how it has developed over the years – exemplify how engagement with specific community groups might occur and be facilitated, and how objections to this practice might be met; these considerations are

DOI: 10.4324/9781003229742-5

crucial in order for any primary school classics project to have meaningful impact in and beyond the classroom.

5.1.1 Engaging with learners and teachers: from transaction to co-creation

When I started my first project, *Literacy through Classics*, I had en-
visaged and planned a clear-cut linear transaction: students would
receive training by me to deliver set content as experts while pupils
received knowledge which would 'help' them in their lives – teachers
would be present in class, but primarily for classroom management.
Reflecting on this now, I am rather self-conscious of my naive and
unwittingly condescending approach, maintaining traditionally hierarchical power relationships, both between lecturer and student, and
between university and school, by removing any active contribution to
the project from university students, and school pupils and teachers.
But at the time, this was how I understood 'outreach' as it seemed appropriate at university level: literally 'reaching out' to wider communities to share academic knowledge. As is now clear, collaboration with
my students, discussions with teachers, and pupil feedback of course
had the most profound impact on the project and indeed on me as
a researcher, and a more accurate term to describe the cooperation
with anyone beyond university is 'community engagement', which at
least allows for active and equal participation of all those involved.[2]
I had particularly overlooked the role of pupils as 'active agents' in
the development of the project.[3] Yet their engagement with – and occasional resistance to – the project has been key, as they continue to
shape the project's conceptualization and content through their input
and feedback.

This awareness took me a while to reach. It was only when one
of my students in Swansea created a 'Roman senate game' in which
every pupil played the role of a senator having to ask for money from
the emperor to start certain building projects,[4] and I did not see
how this activity might possibly work, that I started to understand
the co-creative nature of the project. As the student seemed to trust
the format, and I trusted the student, I decided to let the activity go
ahead. When I visited the classroom during this particular exercise
and saw how pupils engaged wholeheartedly with the game through
confident spoken Latin communication, I first realized that the project
was growing beyond my input, through engagement between students,
pupils, and indeed teachers, and that I might learn from them, and
they from each other, as much as they from me. An obvious lesson,

but nonetheless important to point out. My awareness of this four-way learning in the project transformed my initially linear and hierarchical approach into a reflective practice based on a collaborative approach. Indeed, neither 'students', 'pupils', nor 'teachers' can be considered as static or uniform identities receptively waiting to be taught. Since both teacher priorities (based on curriculum and educational policy shifts) as well as student and pupil interests and abilities differ from year to year, they can be more usefully considered as 'mediated and dynamic' partners.[5] I know I have spoken about co-creation when discussing the didactic approach of the project in Chapter 3, but in fact primary school classics projects can only be truly transformative when they are co-creative in nature. Students, teachers, and pupils all bring innovation into the classroom by means of their unique input. Whether you are a primary or secondary school teacher, university student or secondary school pupil, policymaker or charity coordinating a primary school classics project, working with different stakeholders as a team means everyone's creative input can be facilitated based on their specific skill sets and interests. Collaboration with partner organizations can indeed bring new skills into a project. When the National Museum of Antiquities of Leiden, for example, contacted me about creating object-based ancient Greek lessons, I was ecstatic, since I am neither a historian nor an archaeologist, and their expertise on object-based learning – creatively implemented by Leiden and Ghent University students – brought a new element to the project on which I had little prior expertise. Letting go of the need to control each aspect of a primary school classics project when working with different partner organizations can be quite a task, but from my personal experience, I know it can enrich the project for all participants.

While most students, teachers, and pupils are receptive to the concept of the *Literacy through Classics* and *Young Heroes* projects, there has always been a small number of participants from all three groups who resist engagement. Yet their resistance is as valuable as the enthusiasm of the majority of participants. Sometimes the actual practice of the project overcomes their resistance. I have worked with teachers who were forced to take part in my project by their school and who told me with arms crossed that they did not see any point in their pupils learning a dead language (more on this below); yet by the end of the lessons, they were fully on board. One pupil in a Swansea Latin course was so resistant that they had actually insisted to the teacher they be allowed to read a book in another classroom during the lesson. When my students and I discussed this and I tried to comfort my students by saying it is impossible to reach every child and they should not feel bad about it, their response was: 'We'll make the lessons so exciting that they won't be able to resist'. Week after week, my students reported to me that they saw the pupil dropping their resistance. The pupil would start lingering in class when lessons started, start asking questions about the activities about to take place, and start listening to their classmates when they spoke about how amazing the lessons were. Towards the end of the course, the pupil gave up their resistance entirely and not only stayed in the classroom but took an active part in lessons.[6] When the nature of the project allows for biases and stereotypes in people's minds to be transformed, whether they be teachers, pupils, students, or indeed the coordinator's own, it is the best feeling. However, occasionally when participants resist course content for good reason, such as in the examples of the painful pedagogy I discussed in Chapter 3, the project itself must be transformed, as both the coordinator and other participants search for alternative approaches or exercises.

For anyone interested in primary school classics teaching, reflection on your approach to the people you work with – whether it be hierarchical or collaborative, static or dynamic, transaction-based or co-creative – will help you remain aware of how you frame and develop learning for all those involved, from pupils and students to teachers and academics. Not upholding a strict binary distinction between teacher and learner is the best advice I would give anyone starting on community engagement. For any errors made, and biases experienced, by whichever participant/s can then be transformative learning opportunities for everyone rather than mere mistakes, and meaningful progress is possible.

5.1.2 Engaging with families and communities: taking classics home

Pupils and teachers, however, do not exist in a vacuum, but engage with a complex network of social groups within and outside of school. My projects immediately started having impact beyond the school gates, but I remained largely unaware of this – apart from occasional emails from parents or grandparents thanking us for the lovely course – until I started using questionnaires to gauge the impact of the project. What questionnaires indeed revealed, year after year, is that many pupils are discussing the course content and significance with grandparents, parents, and siblings at home, or with friends.[7] Once I became aware of this, my students and I discussed which activities might engage communities outside of the classroom more explicitly through the pupils. Craft activities are an easy way for pupils to take their results home to share, and homework encourages children to discuss and demonstrate what they are learning with others. I have experimented with various other formats throughout the years: sometimes family have been invited to come to the first or final lesson, other times my students worked on cards for festive holidays which pupils could hand to their parents, or little pots to take home to spark conversation; the 'language passport' I discussed in Chapter 4 is another example.[8] These activities are designed so pupils might have the opportunity to embed their Latin or ancient Greek learning – which tends to be rare in their context – in their wider community. Whom they decide to engage in this conversation is up to them, which can be a transformative learning experience in itself, as pupils now have agency in sharing with others knowledge generally perceived as difficult which they have acquired.

I know that, in my own project, there is much potential left untapped in engaging the communities in which the children taking part in our courses grow up. I would like to have the opportunity to talk to children's families to see how they, in their own words, feel about, and provide input into, their child's Latin or ancient Greek learning. However, not every step can be taken at once. That these communities are becoming aware that their children have the right and the capacity to study Latin or ancient Greek, and that pupils feel the knowledge is now theirs to share with others, is valuable in itself. For anyone setting out on this path of community engagement, I think it is vital to acknowledge that any project will ripple through a community in unseen ways which are difficult to track. Social groups outside of school can be challenging to reach, making communication regarding their engagement with the project rare. Just as I said about the pupils themselves, moreover, family and friends pupils engage with do not belong to a static and merely receptive group either, and it is clear from pupil feedback that family responses to the project can differ widely. While most pupils report family members being interested and providing additional input into pupils' Latin or ancient Greek learning, (luckily rare) negative family feedback may create an emotive barrier impeding pupils' engagement in lessons. This is therefore an important aspect of community engagement to monitor for various reasons. For those readers interested in future practice of classics at primary school, I would recommend considering how you might encourage pupils to embed their learning in their communities. Questionnaires or group interviews might help gauge the ripples caused by the project.[9]

5.1.3   Engaging with the media and policymakers: from pedagogy to practice-based research

Research was not part of the original project aims of my UK project. However, as the number of schools with which we collaborated increased, (head) teachers started asking for information to demonstrate to parents, school governors, and the inspectorate that they were right to set aside time for Latin each week. They wanted to gauge how pupils were impacted by the project, and what evidence supported the teaching of classical languages for literacy improvement among native English speakers. Initially, I was quite resistant to the need to justify my subject – I still think the quantitative data only reveal a limited part of the impact of primary school classics – and would have probably left it at that, had it not been for a 'good news story' which a Welsh TV station wanted to present on the project. It was fantastic: reporters came to the project launch and interviewed pupils, and the general public were asked for their opinion on classics teaching, which sparked a healthy debate. At the end of the news item, however, my heart sank, as they finished along the lines of 'this is all good and well, but both parents and teachers will be wondering what the actual benefits are of their children learning Latin'. It took me a good week to get over what I experienced as a painful public embarrassment – in the end, I decided they were probably right, and that I needed to get this information together to benefit everyone involved.

I have since learned that the media have a tendency towards confirmation bias, in that they look for ways to present classics, Latin, and/or Greek in a way that corroborates their current view of it. When I first explained the *Young Heroes* project to a reporter, I emphasized that pupils did not have to learn anything by rote; however, when I got a draft of the article, the title read something like 'Primary school pupils will now also rote learn ancient Greek words' (by which they implied 'as well as secondary school pupils'). I was flabbergasted. Luckily, I was able to correct the article which was subsequently printed more accurately. Since it is still a novelty in most countries, teaching classics at primary school is likely to attract media attention. Insisting on receiving a draft publication before anything goes out can avoid any glaring misinterpretations. But in spite of this slight note of caution, working together with the media can provide great opportunities to share community engagement with a broader audience. Having Karrewiet, the children's news on Flemish national TV, dedicate an item to *Young Heroes* and interviewing some of the pupils was a wonderful way to start a broader conversation about who Latin and ancient Greek is for, and spark interest among other young people. Indeed, for my own projects, almost every mention in the media has led to interest from new partner organizations and further developments of the project.

No matter how shaken I was by the Welsh TV incident, it did spark my interest in research. I started collating findings from the questionnaires pupils filled in each year and a Leverhulme/BA Small Research Grant allowed me – among other things – to review existing research on the impact of Latin and Greek teaching.[10] This research not only provided me with information to share with partner schools but also altered the nature of the project indefinitely, as research is now an intrinsic part of my work. At Ghent University, I have also researched the impact of the project on literacy,[11] which presented some encouraging results. Research may not be a manageable or possible step to take for everyone interested in teaching classics at primary school, but I would suggest having questionnaires or a class interview at the end of a course as a useful and hopefully achievable way to support personal reflection and gather data for the future.

For a number of years, I used research to support my arguments for teaching Latin at the primary school level in Wales in discussions with head teachers and other local policymakers. In 2015, however, a visit of the Welsh education minister to Swansea University led to my being invited to advise him on a potential role of classics in the new curriculum, which was being devised at that time on the basis of a report by Professor Donaldson (2015). I subsequently wrote two reports for the Welsh government: the first in 2015 on *Learning Latin in Wales: Report on Research and Practice*, the second in 2017 entitled *Classical antiquity as part of the Humanities Area of Learning and Experience in the new Welsh curriculum*.[12] I left the UK before the new curriculum came into being, but was delighted to hear Latin and ancient Greek have been included in the new primary school curriculum among 'international languages', opening up new opportunities for pupils in Wales.

While it may not be possible for everyone interested in teaching Latin or ancient Greek at primary school to think outside of the classroom – indeed, that is how I started – and research or policy engagement are certainly not vital aspects, it may be a useful exercise to envisage how different stakeholders (such as families and wider communities) might provide new input and a richness of experience to any project.

5.2 Community resistance to classics and how to respond to it

There is, however, one major issue which anyone teaching classics at primary school will encounter at some point. I have mentioned this throughout the previous chapters but have not yet elaborated on it. I am talking about bias against classics, concerning its supposed target group, difficulty level, and usefulness. Classics is still stereotyped (even if this is not always correct in the practice of certain projects) as both elitist and useless and hence – as I discussed in Chapter 1 – able to convey social status. This position is further exacerbated by the engagement with classics by people on various points of the political spectrum, such as extremist groups storming the US Capitol building in the guise of Spartan warriors, or traditionalist politicians seeking a united Europe through shared heritage.[13] The problem is that this stereotypical image of classics causes resistance when you set out to offer Latin or ancient Greek to non-traditional target groups: among every stakeholder group involved in primary school classics – teachers and pupils, parents and peers, policy makers and external partners such as university staff – negative stereotypes about classics at primary school exist. This bias usually reveals itself early on in any widening participation project, both before and upon entering the classroom. It is important to be aware of the biased assertions you may come across or unconsciously hold yourself, so I list four objections to classics at primary school which I have come across regularly from different stakeholders.

5.2.1 *You'd be better off teaching pupils more [insert national languagels of your country]*

An understandable point about the seemingly bizarre application of Latin or ancient Greek to improve literacy. However, the reality is that literacy levels worldwide continue to be under pressure,[14] particularly among disadvantaged young people, and traditional methods of teaching more explicit literacy tuition do not always work.[15] Results of US, UK, and German studies as well as my own, which particularly emphasize a positive impact of Latin or ancient Greek study on literacy in English, Spanish, German, and Dutch literacy, might therefore help nuance this objection.

5.2.2 *You'd be better off teaching them Chinese*

A utilitarian point about the impracticality of learning Latin or ancient Greek in an education system driven by a global market economy, made again recently in two separate newspaper articles which mentioned *Young Heroes.* One of the articles states: '[T]his [project] demonstrates what good education can achieve: loving attention and belief in pupils' abilities will always work. The teacher could have probably taught poetry, or Chinese, or architecture.'[16] The other echoes: 'Does this experiment say anything about the use or value of Latin or ancient Greek, or just about the strong image of classical languages? Could children not also feel better from Chinese lessons?'[17] I do not know why Chinese is so often singled out as the exemplary polar opposite to Latin and ancient Greek – because it is considered equally difficult yet incredibly useful in the light of the global economy? Whatever the reason, I am sure the authors of these articles are correct: you would be able to inspire children by teaching them any of these subjects and raise pupils' self-esteem. I do not view ancient languages in competition with Chinese or any other subject. Having said that, the entanglement of classics in the educational inequity issue of access, as well as the function of classics as symbolic signifier of a high social status, as discussed in Chapter 1, is most prevalent in Europe and the US. Chinese, by contrast, is not a standard subject on the secondary school curriculum, meaning that there is no issue of certain social groups having more or less access. While I am for teaching more poetry, architecture, or indeed Chinese, the unique status as cultural capital renders Latin and ancient Greek – at least in Europe and the US – valuable tools for working towards social justice in education.

5.2.3 It's just not for these pupils

This is also an argument I meet regularly, based on a traditional notion of the target group and difficulty level of classics at school. I have met (head) teachers and policymakers who did not see the point of teaching classics to their specific pupil groups. I have also, in the past, heard from my students that they were warned about specific pupils in a class group, since a teacher was unconvinced that particular pupils would be able to 'get' it. This is bias based on the person's opinion of the cognitive abilities of particular pupils as well as the traditional status of classical languages. It is understandable, particularly from a teacher's point of view, when they know to what extent certain pupils *tend* to engage. The statement is usually linked to 'it's too difficult for them' – and yes, if Latin or ancient Greek were taught from the traditional approaches most popular at secondary school, I agree these subjects would not be accessible for everyone. This is why it is pivotal to go beyond mere widening participation and reframe what we mean by Latin or ancient Greek (at secondary school level too). Teaching either language with an adapted pedagogy can indeed offer a 'desirable difficulty' for pupils who are traditionally excluded from the subjects.[18] Since learning Latin and ancient Greek is effortful but the didactic adaptations make the effort available for all, this balanced difficulty level encourages children to develop curiosity and grow.[19] I have yet to meet a pupil who did not engage constructively with our Latin or ancient Greek lessons in some way, and even resistant (head) teachers and policymakers have become supportive of my projects after seeing them in action. But perhaps it is necessary to reformulate the adage 'classics is for everyone' into 'classics *can be* for everyone'.

5.2.4 Pupils will be disappointed when they want to study classics at secondary school and aren't smart enough

In theory, it is possible that this might happen. However, in practice it has never yet occurred, possibly because the pupils my project targets are so far removed from a classics trajectory at secondary school that taking part in the course does not change their educational pathway. The aim of my projects is, indeed, not to prepare pupils for secondary school classics: the courses are about access in the here and now, not access to subjects in the future. The story I mentioned earlier, that I heard from the head teacher of one of our schools that pupils were still talking about the project two years later, when they were in the B-stream of Flemish education, demonstrates that the increase in pupils' academic self-esteem is not connected to them studying classics at secondary school. Learning a societally valued subject such as Latin or ancient Greek is challenging for pupils growing up in deprived circumstances. Asking them to give these subjects a go means encouraging them to choose not only curiosity but also the cognitive and emotional vulnerability that comes with it, of not knowing, of being challenged, of broadening their horizons. If we ask this of them, it is only right that we too choose vulnerability as to the unknowability of how the course will shape specific pupils specifically.

That does not mean I would not like more pupils to study classics at secondary school, and I do think much can be done to increase access for broader pupil groups. Classics at primary school can be – and is already – taught in order to raise awareness among pupils and teachers of classics at secondary school. However, if the aim is to teach classics to improve educational equity, a balance needs to be struck between teaching that is accessible for all participants yet also stimulating for those who are interested in pursuing classics at secondary school. It is also essential that a link is created between primary and secondary school classics learning, so pupils can be included at both levels.

In short, it is useful to be aware of existing stereotypes regarding classics when offering it to non-traditional target groups such as primary school pupils, as they can certainly be bypassed. From experience I know most resistant parties are convinced by the actual practice, so I avoid any 'hard sell' of classics but let the project talk for itself. What I have learned, however, is that difficult communication at the start of a collaboration does not usually bode well for further cooperation. Being clear about the required commitment and the role of each partner in the project can avoid drama later on.

5.3 Conclusion and reflection tools

I hope this section has provided some insight into the different communities you might encounter both inside and outside of the classroom when teaching Latin or ancient Greek at primary school, and how engagement with them might be understood and facilitated. This is not done for its own sake – 'reaching out' – but to ensure that the voice the children find within the classroom is acknowledged and embedded in their social context. This brings us full circle to my starting point of the book, namely that some children do not have the same opportunities as others because of their socioeconomic context. If we only engage with the pupils in our classroom, our practice may be impactful, but in order to facilitate pupils' transformative learning, which entails application of new insights in daily life, we also need to support them in carrying this new-found knowledge into the world outside of the classroom. I do not think I have found all of the answers yet with regard to this community engagement practice, but it is by taking small steps that a path is made.

To finish this chapter, I offer some tools for reflection for the final time (Table 5.1). The answer categories have the following key:

- − −   This is definitely not a priority for me.
- −   I pay attention to this from time to time.
- − +   I would like to pay more attention to this, but I'm not sure how.
- +   I regularly pay attention to this.
- + +   This is an integral part of my current thinking.

Table 5.1 Reflection tools

	– –	–	– +	+	+ +
I am aware of my approach to teaching and engaging with project partners, whether hierarchical or collaborative, static or dynamic, transaction-based or co-creative.					
I create ways for pupils to engage in meaningful dialogue about their classroom learning beyond the classroom.					
I take steps to include families and social networks in my pupils' learning.					
(I understand the pitfalls and opportunities which arise when engaging with the media.)					
(I am able to envisage speaking with local policymakers who might be interested in my work with pupils.)					
I can see how different stakeholders/ project partner organizations might provide new input and a richness of experience to my current teaching practice.					
I understand the role bias (also my own) towards classics plays in its accessibility at primary school level, and how objections against it might be appreciated and nuanced.					

Notes

1 In these two initial aims, the *Literacy through Classics* was, incidentally, successful. Both the acceptance rate of our students on teacher trainee programmes, and awareness in South Wales of classics, increased. On the value of employability at Higher Education, see Barrow et al. 2010.
2 It is well documented (e.g. Staley 2017: 158) that community engagement impacts on researchers, and engagement with schools indeed altered my 'priorities, values, and attitudes' profoundly.
3 Mahony & Stephansen 2017: 47.

4 See http://literacythroughclassics.weebly.com/blog/acting-out-the-senate for the student's blog post.
5 Mahony and Stephansen 2017: 35 argue this about the notion of the 'public'.
6 For a student blog post narrating a similar story, see http://literacythroughclassics.weebly.com/blog/finally-a-breakthrough.
7 Bracke 2021: 392.
8 See pp. 88-89.
9 See https://www.oudegriekenjongehelden.ugent.be/en/teaching-materials/course-1-monsters-in-storytelling-traditions/lesson-5-a-heros-journey/ for the English-medium questionnaire.
10 Bracke 2016 and Bracke & Bradshaw 2021.
11 See pp. 33-35.
12 Both reports can be read online: Bracke 2015a and 2017a.
13 Pharos 2021, De Pourcq 2019, Mac Sweeney et al. 2019.
14 Study International 2019.
15 See p. 24.
16 Truijens 2022.
17 Ruyters 2022.
18 D'Mello & Graesser 2014: 306.
19 Brown 2022: Chapter 4.

Conclusion

The title of my book is 'Classics at primary school: a tool for social justice', and I would argue that it is indeed possible to use the study of Latin or ancient Greek languages and cultures to improve educational equity, a key factor in working towards social justice as outlined in Chapter 1. Educational equity work does not only mean providing more equal educational access and opportunities for pupils but also treating them more equally within the education system.[1] US and UK primary school projects from the past decades have led the way in demonstrating how the study of classics may empower pupils, using a variety of didactic approaches, course formats, and teachers (ranging from university students to retirees). I myself have contributed to UK practice through my *Literacy through Classics* project, and through the Flemish *Ancient Greeks – Young Heroes* project further developed my understanding of educational equity through classics and how we might work towards it. Having outlined my personal approach in the previous chapters, it is now possible to draw some conclusion about its successes and challenges, and think ahead to potential future practice.

It is clear that all of the projects I have discussed in this book which make Latin or ancient Greek accessible for non-traditional target groups have been able to empower children, raise their aspirations, and improve their literacy in the school language. There is sufficient evidence for this by now, as I demonstrated in the first two chapters. When I consider the questionnaires of my own project, which pupils fill in at the end of each course,[2] the high satisfaction levels – both for different aspects of the project, such as learning about stories and engagement with the student-teachers, as well as for the project as a whole – confirm that my students' lessons have a positive impact on pupils. Many children connect on an emotional level to the subject matter and the university students. One child in our latest course wrote a PS at the end of their questionnaire: 'I thought the lessons were super

DOI: 10.4324/9781003229742-6

fun I'm so sorry they're already over I'll miss you taught such nice lessons' (*sic*).[3] The questionnaires also reveal that many children talk to their family and friends about the lessons.[4] Their reasons for communicating about their learning experience vary, as one pupil stated, 'I talk to my family because I enjoy learning another language', while another says, 'I explain to my parents, my brother, my sister, and my best friends what we have done in each lesson'. Parents are engaged in dialogue the most: one child told us 'I speak to my mum about the [ancient Greek] letters', while another talks 'to [his] dad about how much fun it was'. The majority of children who take part in the project want to share their knowledge with their family and social circle, which corroborates that the project is about more than just language learning for pupils: it is about being known and seen to learn something difficult, and having a voice by taking an active part in the knowledge creation process and sharing this knowledge with others. My research (outlined in Chapter 2) also reveals that pupils' reading comprehension improves significantly in comparison with control groups, over the course of just five weeks. These are encouraging findings by themselves regarding the educational and linguistic empowerment of the children who take part in the project.

I would argue that the reason for the positive impact of the *Young Heroes* project is its particular educational practice. This has, throughout the years, aimed at improving educational equity in three interconnected ways: first, by offering a traditionally inaccessible subject to children who would not normally encounter it in their curriculum ('widening participation', discussed in Chapter 2); secondly, by adapting the pedagogy so children start to find their voice in the knowledge co-creation process of classics, and are invited to transform limiting beliefs about themselves (Chapters 3 and 4); and thirdly, by embedding pupils' learning into their communities (Chapter 5). But to what extent does this combination of factors contribute towards educational equity? I would argue that pupil empowerment is key in working towards educational equity as it enables children to take responsibility for their own learning and world view; however, I would propose that it is not the only required factor, and that the success of *Young Heroes* lies in the fact that it works towards changing limiting beliefs among all participants and stakeholders involved. In order to gauge the impact of the project on educational equity, we therefore need to consider how it affects both the education system and its participants.

Let us first have a look at all of the participants of the education system. Going into schools, talking to (head) teachers or parents, my students and I regularly run into the same message: 'It's not for them.' Certain pupils get pointed out: 'They won't get it.' Sometimes children have internalized this message and tell us themselves: 'This is too difficult for me'. Bias is not something we have tried to capture in our questionnaires, but it comes through loud and clear at the start of each new course in spoken communication. My students are trained to be aware of it, which makes them respond in a constructive manner, though they come into the classroom with their own biases, often about what it entails to study 'classics' and how it should be taught. And so the first aspect of the project's educational practice – widening participation in classics – already offers a disorienting experience for many of those involved. The transformative learning potential of our courses is, however, only activated through the lessons themselves, because it is as pupils progress through the course that we see participants' views changing: my university students learn how to make their lesson content and didactic material accessible, pupils who had been given up on at the start of the course start to blossom, and teachers' perceptions of certain pupils' capacities may be re-evaluated. I have less information on families and parents rethinking their understanding of their child's cognitive capacities, but that they are being drawn into the conversation means the potential for a reassessment of their child's cognitive capacities is at least present. It is hence the lessons themselves – the second aspect of my educational practice: adapted pedagogy – which offer the potential for transformative learning among all participants. I do think the teacher is key here, and that any committed teacher using an inclusive pedagogy would be able to work towards transformative learning.[5] However, I hope Chapters 3 and 4 have provided discussions of approaches, techniques, and exercises which I have personally experienced – and have found in other projects – work (or do not work) in this context. This disruption of pupils', teachers', and parents' perceived limitations is vital when working towards educational equity, because as I argued in Chapter 1, children do not generally have control over, and are not responsible for, the circumstances in which they grow up. We must therefore also engage the communities around them, which is the third aspect of my educational practice ('community engagement'). Indeed, while I would argue that our children's education must be central when we want to work towards a more equitable world, children's classroom learning must be embedded in their home situation so any positive changes in pupils' mindsets can be contextualized.

By disrupting limiting beliefs and bias from the bottom-up, working towards educational equity is possible at a local level. As more schools and teachers become familiar with the online teaching materials and our didactic approach, and become aware that ancient Greek is accessible for their pupils, the definition of 'classics' and the common perception of its target audience is slowly starting to change. A number of primary schools in Flanders now incorporate the *Young Heroes* lesson materials into the curriculum – increasing access to classics themselves, without university input – and secondary schools too have started to offer ancient Greek to non-traditional target groups, and comment on the positive impact the project has on pupils. In this way, the project also contributes positively to the academic field of 'classics' as well as to the general conception of our education systems.

While the *Young Heroes* certainly knows the successes I have just outlined, many practical and systemic challenges remain. Practically, the project is limited in scope, runs on a small budget (I currently spend around €300–500 each year on teaching materials and travel reimbursement), and depends primarily on my initiative. My own learning is, moreover, cyclical in nature, as I create, reshape, scrap, and reinvent activities with a new group of students on an annual basis. Writing this book has also made me aware of gaps in my current practice: in the future, I am therefore keen to go into dialogue better with children's families, focus on supporting boys' literacy particularly, and offer a school year-long course. Systemically, moreover, two major challenges often frustrate me. First, that the Flemish school curriculum does not have official guidelines with regard to classics at primary school sometimes makes it seem like classics has been pushed to the margins of education.[6] Also, when we do innovative work at primary school level, it can be discouraging to see the gap between primary and secondary school, where Latin and ancient Greek are still largely the reserve of a small group.[7] There are nevertheless ways to rethink these systemic challenges. The marginalization of classics also means primary school is precisely where we may innovate and find ways to intervene in children's downward spiral of decreasing aspirations in order to empower them. Closing the gap between primary and secondary school is difficult, but I think the way forward lies in small projects making incremental changes at a local level, rather than a big overhaul of the education system. When we consider past and current primary school classics projects, a picture of incremental change in the face of systemic barriers in fact emerges. Current innovations in classics pedagogy, local and international collaborations between different levels of education, a fast-moving integration of digital learning, and other developments in our approach to classics make me optimistic about a future for classics at primary school.

Not all of my readers will be interested in starting a primary school classics project, but I hope you nonetheless found the reflection process on your personal educational practice or policy (past, present, or future) useful. For those of you interested in stepping onto the road less travelled and offering classics at primary school, I trust the different chapters in this book have offered some practical guidance in taking the next steps. You will, of course, have different interests and expertise compared to me, and as I have emphasized throughout the book, local solutions are needed to address the needs of pupils growing up in particular regions or countries. While it is your own reflection process which will shape your personal educational practice, I hope the practical guidelines I have given in Chapters 3 and 4 will be of use.

Making classics accessible for non-traditional target groups is by definition a work-in-progress, as educational equity is – at least in our current education systems – something we can only work towards, not actually attain. In this context, classics can only ever be an imperfect tool, as it is also just one social and educational gatekeeper, and not everyone can be reached through it: not all limiting beliefs can be disrupted, not all biases transformed. We can rather use the beauty and challenge we ourselves find in Latin or ancient Greek to offer to pupils – and, through them, the communities around them – the opportunity for positive change. It may seem challenging to gauge this impact, as pupils respond to the lessons in different ways, are interested in different aspects, and any of the participants (not just the pupils) may indeed get to grips with their experience of the project at different points, perhaps even long after the project has ended. Further research on both practice and policy may provide supplementary evidence, yet will never paint a complete picture: for me, the value of the practice is crystal clear. In spite of limitations and challenges, I am confident – and I hope you agree with me – that primary school classics can be applied as a valuable tool in the bigger picture of working towards educational equity.

Notes

1 Nicaise 2000: 38. See also Chapter 1, p. 9.
2 See Chapter 2.
3 My translation of the Dutch.
4 See Chapter 5.
5 See also Hunt 2022: Introduction.
6 See pp. 26-28.
7 See pp. 12-13.

Bibliography

Barrow, R. et al. (2010). Embedding employability into a Classics curriculum: The Classical Civilisation Bachelor of Arts programme at Roehampton University. *Arts and Humanities in Higher Education, 9*(3), 339–52.

Bassman, M., Ironsmith, M. (1984). An experimental FLES program in Latin. *ADFL Bulletin, 16*, 41.

Beck, V., Hahn, H., Lepenies, R. (eds.) (2020). Interdisciplinary perspectives on poverty measurement, epistemic injustices and social activism. In *Dimensions of poverty: Measurement, epistemic injustices, activism* (pp. 1–22). Springer.

Beke, W. (2020). *Vlaams actieplan armoedebestrijding 2020–2024*. Vlaamse Overheid. https://www.vlaanderen.be/publicaties/vlaams-actieplan-armoede bestrijding-2020-2024.

Bell, B. (1999). *Minimus: Starting out in Latin*. Cambridge University Press.

———— (2004). *Minimus Secundus: Moving on in Latin*. Cambridge University Press.

Bell, B., Wing-Davey, Z. (2018). Delivering Latin in primary schools. In A. Holmes-Henderson, S. Hunt, M. Musié (eds.) (pp. 111–27).

Benson, M., Bridge, G., Wilson, D. (2015). School choice in London and Paris – A comparison of middle-class strategies. *Social Policy & Administration, 49*, 24–43.

Bigiman, K. (2022). *It mare proruptum*. Een gymnasiumopleiding in Amsterdam-Zuidoost. In E. Huig, I. Kuin, M. Liebregts (eds.), *De huid van Cleopatra: Etniciteit en diversiteit in de oudheidstudies* (pp. 240–49). Verloren.

Blanquer, J.-M. et al. (2021). *Déclaration conjointe des ministres européens chargés de l'éducation visant à renforcer la coopération européenne autour du latin et du grec ancien*. Ministère de l'éducation nationale, de la jeunesse et des sports. https://eduscol.education.fr/document/12640/download?attachment.

Bond, S.E. (2019, 20 December). How to kill a canon: Sourcebooks that address the silence. *Society for Classical Studies*. https://classicalstudies.org/ scs-blog/sarah-e-bond/blog-how-kill-canon-sourcebooks-address-silence.

Bonod, L. (2021, 14 September). Les langues anciennes, décimées en silence au lycée. *Le Monde*. https://www.lemonde.fr/societe/article/2021/09/14/les-langues-anciennes-decimees-en-silence-au-lycee_6094564_3224.html.

Boone, S. (2011). *Sociale ongelijkheid bij de overgang van basis- naar secundair onderwijs: Een onderzoek naar de oriënteringspraktijk.* Vlaams ministerie van Onderwijs en Vorming.

Bostick, D. (2021). The classical roots of white supremacy. *Learning for Justice.* https://www.learningforjustice.org/magazine/spring-2021/the-classical-roots-of-white-supremacy.

Bourdieu, P. (1986). The forms of capital. In J. Richardson (ed.), *Handbook of theory and research for the sociology of education.* Greenward Press.

Bracey, J. (2017, 12 October). Why students of color don't take Latin. *Eidolon.* https://eidolon.pub/why-students-of-color-dont-take-latin-4ddee3144934.

Bracke, E. (2010). *Of metis and magic: The conceptual transformations of Circe and Medea in ancient Greek poetry.* [Unpublished PhD thesis]. Maynooth University.

—— (2015). Bringing ancient languages into a modern classroom: Some reflections. *Journal of Classics Teaching, 32,* 35–39.

—— (2015a). Learning Latin in Wales: Report on research and practice. *Swansea University.* https://www.oudegriekenjongehelden.ugent.be/wp-content/uploads/2020/06/Bracke-Learning-Latin-in-Wales.pdf.

—— (2016). The role of university student teachers in increasing Widening Participation to classics. *Journal of Widening Participation and Lifelong Learning, 18*(2), 111–29.

—— (2017). Naar een democratisering van klassieke talenonderwijs? Praktische voorbeelden van differentiatie en dekolonisatie uit het Verenigd Koninkrijk. *Prora, 22*(2), 16–22.

—— (2017a). Classical antiquity as part of the humanities area of learning and experience in the new Welsh curriculum. *Swansea University.* https://www.oudegriekenjongehelden.ugent.be/wp-content/uploads/2020/06/Evelien-Bracke-Classics-in-Humanities-report.pdf.

—— (2021). 'Iedereen Latijn' van theorie naar praktijk: Een diversiteitstoolkit. *Didactica Classica Gandensia, 54,* 49–74.

Bracke, E., Bradshaw, C. (2020). The impact of learning Latin on school pupils: A review of existing data. *Language Learning Journal, 48*(2), 226–36.

Brookfield, S. (2012). *Teaching for critical thinking: Tools and methods to help students question their assumptions.* Jossey-Bass.

Brown, B. (2022). *Atlas of the heart: Mapping meaningful connection and the language of human experience.* Random House.

Bulwer, J. (ed.) (2006). *Classics teaching in Europe.* Bloomsbury.

—— (2018). Changing priorities in classics education in mainland Europe. In A. Holmes-Henderson, S. Hunt, M. Musié (eds.) (pp. 67–88).

Burns, K.E. (2018). Marginalization of local varieties in the L2 classroom: The case of U.S. Spanish. *L2 Journal, 10*(1), 20–38.

Butin, D. (2007). Justice-learning: Service-learning as justice-oriented education. *Equity and Excellence in Education, 40*(2), 177–83.

Butler, T., Hamnett, C. (2007). The geography of education: Introduction. *Urban Studies, 44*(7), 1161–74.

Butterworth, E. (2017). Latin in the community: The Paideia Institute's Aequora program. *Classical Outlook, 92*(1), 2–8.

Caterine, M. (2018). *Non sibi, sed suis*: Service-Learning in Advanced Latin Courses. *Classical Outlook, 93*(3), 97–105.

Cederstrom, E. (1974). *Quid agunt discipuli?* Latin in Philadelphia. *Independent School Bulletin, 33*, 56–57.

Center for Faculty Excellence (2004). Managing classroom conflict. *CFE University of North Carolina at Chapel Hill, 22*, 1–4.

Chanock, K. (2006). Help for a dyslexic learner from an unlikely source: The study of Ancient Greek. *Literacy* 40, 164–170.

Crabtree, S., Kluch, S. (2020, 5 March). How many women worldwide are single moms? *Gallup.* https://news.gallup.com/poll/286433/women-worldwide-single-moms.aspx.

Crenshaw, K. (1989). Demarginalizing the intersection of race and sex: A black feminist critique of antidiscrimination doctrine, feminist theory and antiracist politics. *University of Chicago Legal Forum,* 139–68.

D'Mello, S., Graesser, A.C. (2014). Confusion. In R. Pekrun, L. Linnenbrink-Garcia (eds.), *International handbook of emotions in education* (pp. 289–310). Routledge.

Dalley, S. (1991). Gilgamesh in the *Arabian Nights. Journal of the Royal Asiatic Society, 1*(1), 1–17.

De Backer, F. et al. (2020). Functional use of multilingualism in assessment: Opportunities and challenges. *Research Notes (Cambridge Assessment English), 78*, 35–43.

Delaney, et al. (2021). Keeping the ancient world relevant for modern students with *Suburani. Journal of Classics Teaching, 43*, 64–67.

De Pourcq, M. (2019). The costly fabric of conservatism: Classical references in contemporary public culture. In Richardson (ed.) (pp. 171–83).

Derks, A., Vermeersch, H. (2001). *Gender en schools presteren: Een multilevel-analyse naar de oorzaken van de grotere schoolachterstand van jongens in het Vlaams secundair onderwijs.* Tempus Omnia Revelat.

DESA (2006). *Social Justice in an open world: The role of the United Nations.* United Nations.

Dhindsa, H.S. (2020). What studying Classics taught me about my relationship with Western Civilisation. *CUCD*, 49, 1–9.

Donaldson, G. (2015). *Successful futures: Independent review of curriculum and assessment arrangements in Wales.* Welsh Government. https://gov.wales/sites/default/files/publications/2018-03/successful-futures.pdf.

Duchemin, L., Durand, A., Franceschetti, B. (2023). The Nausicaa experience: Introduction to ancient Greek at school in France. *Journal of Classics Teaching.*

Eddy, P.A. (1981). *The effect of foreign language study in high school on verbal ability as measured by the scholastic aptitude test-verbal.* Washington Center for Applied Linguistics.

122 Bibliography

Ennser-Kananen, J. (2016). A pedagogy of pain: New directions for world language education. *Modern Language Journal, 100,* 556–64.

Erner, G. (2021, 17 November). Plan européen pour le latin et le grec: Pourquoi développer l'apprentissage des langues anciennes? *France Culture.* https://www.franceculture.fr/emissions/la-question-du-jour/plan-europeen-pour-le-latin-et-le-grec-pourquoi-developper-l-apprentissage-des-langues-anciennes.

European Commission/EACEA/Eurydice. (2017). *Key data on teaching languages at school in Europe – 2017 Edition. Eurydice Report.* Publications Office of the European Union.

Faya Cerqueiro, F., Chao Castro, M. (2015). Board-games as review lessons in English language teaching: Useful resources for any level. *Docencia e Investigación, 25*(2), 67–82.

Ford, K.A., Maxwell, K. (2013). Identity, power, and conflict: Pedagogical strategies for successful classroom peer dynamics. In M.A. Chesler, A.A. Young (eds.), *Faculty identities and the challenge of diversity.* Routledge.

Franck, E., Nicaise, I. (2019). *Ongelijkheden in het Vlaamse onderwijssysteem: verbetering in zicht? Een vergelijking tussen PISA 2003 en 2015.* HIVA/SONO.

Freire, P. (2005 [1970]). *Pedagogy of the oppressed* (Trans. M. Bergman Ramos). Continuum.

Freund, S., Janssen, L. (eds.) (2017). *Communis lingua gentibus : Interkulturalität und Lateinunterricht.* Speyer.

Fromchuck, A. (1984). The measurable benefits of teaching English through Latin in Elementary School. *Classical World, 78,* 25–29.

Gagarin, M. (2010). *The Oxford encyclopedia of ancient Greece and Rome.* Oxford University Press.

Gager, J.G. (1992). *Curse tablets and binding spells from the ancient world.* Oxford University Press.

García, O. (2019). Translanguaging: A coda to the code? *Classroom Discourse, 10*(3–4), 369–73.

George, E.V. (1998). Latin and Spanish: Roman culture and Hispanic America. In LaFleur (ed.), *Latin for the 21st century: From concept to classroom* (pp. 227–36). Scott Foresman-Addison Wesley.

Gerhards, J., Sawert, T., Kohler, U. (2019). Des Kaisers *alte* Kleider: Fiktion und Wirklichkeit des Nutzens von Lateinkenntnissen. *Kölner Zeitschrift für Soziologie und Sozialpsychologie, 71,* 309–26.

Glynn, C., Wesely, P., Wassell, B. (2014). *Words and actions: Teaching languages through the lens of social justice.* ACTFL.

Godwin-Jones, R. (2014). Games in language learning: Opportunities and challenges. *Language Learning & Technology, 18*(2), 9–19.

Goik, L.-S. (2021). *Zur Wirkung des Lateinunterrichts. Ergebnisse einer Längsschnittstudie.* Logos Verlag.

Goosen, K. et al. (2017). *Is dat iets voor mij juf? Leerlingen versterken in het keuzeproces van basis naar secundair.* Lannoo.

Goossens, C., Muls, J., Van Gorp, A. (2015). Schoolsegregatie als een lappendeken. *Welwijs, 26*(3), 3–6.

Green, F., Kynaston, D. (2019). *Engines of privilege: Britain's private school problem.* Bloomsbury.

Greenwald, A.G., Krieger, L.H. (2006). Implicit bias: Scientific foundations. *California Law Review, 94*(4), 945–67.

Greenwood, E. (2010). *Afro-Greeks: Dialogues between anglophone Caribbean literature and classics in the twentieth century.* Oxford University Press.

Gross Davis, B. (2009). *Tools for teaching,* 2nd edition. Jossey-Bass.

Grosse, M. (2017). *Pons Latinus: Latein als Brücke zum Deutschen als Zweitsprache.* Peter Lang.

Gutacker, B. (1979). Fördert Lateinunterricht sprachliche Fertigkeiten im Deutschen? In K.J. Klauser, H.J. Kornadt (eds.), *Jahrbuch für Empirische Erziehungswissenschaft 1979* (pp. 9–32). Schwann.

Hall, E. (2021). Classics invented: Books, schools, universities and society 1679–1742. In S. Harrison, C. Pelling (eds.), *Classical scholarship and its history: Festschrift for Christopher Stray* (pp. 35–58). De Gruyter.

Hall, E., Stead, H. (2020). *A people's history of classics: Class and Greco-Roman antiquity in Britain and Ireland 1689 to 1939.* Routledge.

Hannan, L. et al. (2013). Object based learning: A powerful pedagogy for higher education. In A. Boddington et al. (eds.), *Museums and Higher Education working together: Challenges and opportunities* (pp. 159–68). Routledge.

Hardwick, L. (2013). Against the 'democratic turn': Counter-texts; counter-contexts; counter-arguments. In L. Hardwick, S.J. Harrison (eds.), *Classics in the modern world: A 'democratic turn?'* (pp. 15–32). Oxford University Press.

Härkönen, J. (2018). Single-mother poverty: How much do educational differences in single motherhood matter? In R. Nieuwenhuis, L.C. Maldonado (eds.), *The triple bind of single-parent families: Resources, employment and policies to improve wellbeing* (pp. 31–50). Bristol University Press.

Hattie, J. (2009). *Visible learning: A synthesis of over 800 meta-analyses relating to achievement.* Routledge.

Heidsieck, L. (2018, 1 October). Latin et grec: Jean-Michel Blanquer veut 'revitaliser' les langues anciennes. *Le Figaro.* https://etudiant.lefigaro.fr/article/latin-et-grec-jean-michel-blanquer-veut-revitaliser-les-langues-anciennes_a7a19532-c54e-11e8-8ab8-0865eb3bb52c/.

Henderson, M. et al. (2020). Private schooling, subject choice, upper secondary attainment and progression to university. *Oxford Review of Education, 46*(3), 295–312.

Hendrickson, T. (2020, 30 January). Gender diversity in Greek and Latin grammar: Ten ancient discussions. *Ad Meliora.* https://medium.com/ad-meliora/gender-diversity-in-greek-and-latin-grammar-ten-ancient-discussions-df371fe19af8.

Hill, B. (2006). Latin for students with severe foreign language learning difficulties. In J. Gruber-Miller (ed.), *When dead tongues speak: Teaching Beginning Greek and Latin* (50–67). Oxford University Press.

Hirsch, J. (2017). *The feedback fix: Dump the past, embrace the future, and lead the way to change.* Rowman & Littlefield.

Holmes, C.T., Keffer, R.L. (2010). A computerized method to teach Latin and Greek root words: Effect on verbal SAT scores. *The Journal of Educational Research, 89*(1), 47–50.

Holmes-Henderson, A. (2023). *Inclusive classics: Innovative pedagogies in museums and schools.* Routledge.

Holmes-Henderson, A., Hunt, S., Musié, M. (eds.) (2018). *Forward with classics: Classical languages in schools and communities.* Bloomsbury.

hooks, b. 1994. *Teaching to transgress: Education as the practice of freedom.* London.

Hubbard, T. (2003). Special Needs in classics. In J. Morwoord (ed.), *The teaching of classics* (pp. 51–60). Cambridge University Press.

Hunt, S. (2016). Teaching sensitive topics in the secondary classics classroom. *Journal of Classics Teaching, 17*(34), 31–43.

———— (2018). Getting classics into schools? Classics and the social justice agenda of the UK coalition government, 2010–2015. In A. Holmes-Henderson, S. Hunt, M. Musié (eds.) (pp. 9–26).

———— (2021). Active Latin teaching for the inclusive classroom. In S. Hunt, M. Lloyd (eds.), *Communicative Approaches for ancient languages* (pp. 55–65).

———— (2022). *Teaching Latin: Contexts, theories, practices.* Bloomsbury.

Hunt, S., Holmes-Henderson, A. (2021). A-level classics poverty. Classical subjects in schools in England. *CUCD Bulletin, 50,* 1–26.

Hwb (2022, 10 January). *Languages, literacy and communication.* Welsh Government. https://hwb.gov.wales/curriculum-for-wales/languages-literacy-and-communication/designing-your-curriculum.

Janoff, R. (2014). The elite meets the street: Teaching Latin in a nonselective Brooklyn Charter School. *Classical World, 107*(2), 258–62.

Jones, P., Sidwell, K. (2016). *Reading Latin. 1. Text and vocabulary. 2. Grammar and exercises,* 2nd edition. Cambridge University Press.

Kahneman, D. (2011). *Thinking, fast and slow.* Farrar, Straus and Giroux.

Kalthoff, H. (2018). *Opgroeien en opvoeden in armoede.* Utrecht.

Karpiak, I. (2006). Chaos and complexity: A framework for understanding social workers at midlife. In V.A. Anfara, N.T. Mertz (eds.), *Theoretical framework in qualitative research* (pp. 85–108). Sage.

Kipf, S. (ed.) (2014). *Integration durch Sprache: Schüler nichtdeutscher Herkunftssprache lernen Latein.* Propylaeum.

———— (2019). Mit Heterogenität produktiv umgehen? Sprachsensibel Latein unterrichten! In M. Keip, T. Dopener (eds.), *Interaktive Fachdidaktik Latein 4* (pp. 77–96). Vandenhoeck & Ruprecht.

Kitchell, K.J. (2014). 'Solitary perfection?' The past, present, and future of elitism in Latin education. In E. Archibald, W. Brockliss, J. Gnoza (eds.), *Learning Latin and Greek from antiquity to the present* (166–83). Cambridge University Press.

Knight, J. (1997). On the extinction of the Japanese wolf. *Asian Folklore Studies, 56*(1), 129–59.

Ko, M. (2000). *Enseigner les langues anciennes*. Hachette Education.

Kuhlmann, P. (2020). Möglichkeiten der Sprachförderung durch Lateinunterricht angesichts einer heterogenen Schülerschaft. *Zeitschrift für Schul- und Professionsentwicklung, 2*(4), 1–10.

Lahaye, W., Pannecoucke, I., Sansen, F. (2019). *Kinderarmoede en het lokale niveau*. Koning Boudewijnstichting.

LeBovit, J. (1967). Qui timide rogat, docet negare. *Classical World, 61*(2), 37–40.

Libatique, D. (2020, 10 August). Object-ifying language: In the classroom, syntax can be a tool or a weapon. *Eidolon*. https://eidolon.pub/object-ifying-language-fd8d3d75cb6f.

Louden, B. (2011). *Homer's Odyssey and the near east*. Cambridge University Press.

MacDonald, E. (2018, 4 October). Warrior women: Despite what gamers might believe, the ancient world was full of female fighters. *The Conversation*. https://theconversation.com/warrior-women-despite-what-gamers-might-believe-the-ancient-world-was-full-of-female-fighters-104343.

Mac Sweeney, N. et al. (2019). Claiming the classical: The Greco-Roman world in contemporary political discourse. *Council of University Classics Departments UK, 48*, 1–19.

Maguire, J. (2018). Latin in Norfolk: Joining up the dots. In A. Holmes-Henderson, S. Hunt, M. Musié (eds.)(pp. 129–36).

Mahony, N., Stephansen, H. (2017). Engaging with the public in public engagement with research. *Research for All, 1*, 35–51.

Masciantonio, R. (1975). Latin for fifth and sixth graders in Easthampton, Massachusetts. *Classical World, 68*, 444.

Mavrogenes, N. (1977). The effect of elementary Latin instruction on language arts performance. *Elementary School Journal, 77*, 268–73.

Merry, M., Boterman, W. (2020). Educational inequality and state-sponsored elite education: The case of the Dutch gymnasium. *Comparative Education, 56*(4), 522–46.

Mezirow, J. (1991). *Transformative dimensions of adult learning*. Jossey-Bass.

Mood, C., Jonsson, J.O. (2016). The social consequences of poverty: An empirical test on longitudinal data. *Social Indicators Research* 127, 633–52.

Nausicaa (2015, 31 May). Pédagogie. A la découverte de Prométhée. *Nausicaa*. http://nausicaa13.free.fr/articles.php?lng=fr&pg=417.

Ndaji, F., Little, J., Coe, R. (2016). *A comparison of academic achievement in Independent and State schools*. Centre for Evaluation and Monitoring, Durham University.

Nicaise, I. et al. (eds.) (2000). *The right to learn: Educational strategies for socially excluded youth in Europe*. Bristol University Press.

Nicaise, I. (2000). Strategies to reduce educational inequality: A general framework. In I. Nicaise et al. (eds.) (pp. 37–50).

Nieto, S. (2010). *Language, culture, and teaching: Critical perspectives*. Routledge.

Northumbria University Newcastle. (2015). *Sound training: Data analysis*. Lexonik. https://lexonik.co.uk/wp-content/uploads/2020/11/Northumbria-University-Study-Lexonik-Full-Data-Analysis.pdf.

Ogbu, J.U. (1988). Cultural diversity and human development. In D.T. Slaughter (ed.), *Black children and poverty: A developmental perspective* (pp. 11–25). Jossey-Bass.

Ogden, D. (2021). *The werewolf in the ancient world*. Oxford University Press.

Ono-dit-Biot, C. (2021, 15 November). Jean-Michel Blanquer: 'la culture ne doit pas être associée aux privilèges d'une élite'. *Le Point*. https://www.lepoint.fr/culture/jean-michel-blanquer-la-culture-ne-doit-pas-etre-associee-aux-privileges-d-une-elite-15-11-2021-2452090_3.php.

Otheguy, R. et al. (2015). Clarifying translanguaging and deconstructing named languages: A perspective from linguistics. *Applied Linguistics Review*, 6(3), 281–307.

Pandey, K.R. (2021). *Theorising transformative learning*. Brill.

Pandey, N. (2021, 15 April). Diversifying classics in Germany: An interview with Katharina Wesselmann. *Society for Classical Studies*. https://classicalstudies.org/scs-blog/nandini-pandey/blog-diversifying-classics-germany-interview-katharina-wesselmann.

Penrose, W.D. (2014). A world away from ours: Homoeroticism in the Classics classroom. In N.S. Rabinowitz, F. McHardy (eds.)(pp. 227–47).

Pharos (2021, 14 January). Capitol terrorists take inspiration from ancient world. *Pharos*. https://pharos.vassarspaces.net/2021/01/14/capitol-terrorists-take-inspiration-from-ancient-world/.

PISA UGent. (2018). *Leesvaardigheid van 15-jarigen*. PISA UGent. https://www.pisa.ugent.be/uploads/files/Vlaamse-resultaten-PISA-2018.pdf.

Polsky, M. (1986). The NEH/Brooklyn college Latin cornerstone project, 1982–84: Genesis, implementation, evaluation. *Classical Outlook, 63*, 77–83.

Quinn, J. (2017, 27 October). Against classics. Women's Classical Committee. https://wcc-uk.blogs.sas.ac.uk/2017/10/27/against-classics/

Rabinowitz, N.S., McHardy, F. (eds.) (2014). *From abortion to pederasty: Addressing difficult topics in the classics classroom*. Ohio State University Press.

Randolph, L.J., Johnson, S.M. (2017). Social Justice in the language classroom: A call to action. *Dimensions*, 99–121.

Reay, D. (2017). *Miseducation: Inequality, education and the working classes*. Bristol University Press.

Richardson, E. (ed.) (2018). *Classics in extremis: The edges of classical reception*. Bloomsbury.

Robinson, L. (2013). *Telling tales in Latin*. Souvenir Press.

——— (2016). *Distant lands: Telling tales in Latin 2*. Souvenir Press.

——— (2017). *Telling tales in Greek*. Souvenir Press.

Robson, J., Lloyd, M. (*forthcoming*). Battling for Latin: Instructors and students on the challenges of teaching and learning beginners' Latin in UK universities. *Classical World*.

Rombaut, K., Cantillon, B., Verbist, G. (2006). *Determinanten van de differentiële slaagkansen in het Hoger onderwijs*. Universiteit Antwerpen, Centrum voor sociaal beleid Herman Deleeck.

Rosiers, K. (2021). Dutch if possible, and also when it's not: The inclusion of multilingualism in declared, perceived and practiced language policies in a Brussels secondary school. In L. Mary, A. Krüger, A. Young (eds.), *Migration, multilingualism and education* (pp. 70–92). Multilingual Matters.

Rosings, A. (2023). Teaching classics at primary school with the help of secondary school pupils. *Journal of Classics Teaching*.

Ross, A. (ed.) (2021). What do educational science and the public good mean in the context of educational research for social justice? In *Educational Research for Social Justice* (pp. 1–26). Springer.

Ruyters, J. (2022). Van wit elitair bolwerk tot creatieve broedplaats: discussie over het gymnasium is er al eeuwen. *Trouw*. https://www.trouw.nl/cultuur-media/van-wit-elitair-bolwerk-tot-creatieve-broedplaats-discussie-over-het-gymnasium-is-er-al-eeuwen~bb286ac1/.

Sawert, T. (2016). Tote Sprachen als lohnende Investition? *Zeitschrift für Soziologie, 45*, 340–36.

———— (2018). *Latente Mechanismen sozialer Hierarchisierung. Die Wahl alter Sprachen als Reproduktionsmechanismus des Bildungsbürgertums*. VS Verlag für Sozialwissenschaften.

Sawyer, B. (2016). Latin for all identities. *Journal of Classics Teaching, 17*(33), 35–39.

School District of Philadelphia. (1970). *How the Romans lived and spoke (Teachers' guide)*. Philadelphia Instructional Services.

Seltzer, K., Wassell, B. (2022). Toward an antiracist world language classroom: A translanguaging approach. *The Language Educator*, Winter, 27–31.

Sheridan, R. (1976). *Augmenting reading skills through language learning transfer. FLES Latin Programme Evaluation Reports*. Indianapolis Public Schools.

Sienkewicz, T.J. et al. (2004). *Lingua Latina Liberis*: Four models for Latin in the elementary school. *Classical Journal, 99*(3), 301–12.

Sierens, S. (2007). *Leren voor diversiteit. Leren in diversiteit*. Steunpunt Diversiteit en Leren, Universiteit Gent.

Singleton, G.E. (2014). *Courageous Conversations about Race*, 2nd edition. Farmington Hills.

Smith, K. (2016, 24 August). Girls may perform better at school than boys – but their experience is much less happy. *The Conversation*. https://theconversation.com/girls-may-perform-better-at-school-than-boys-but-their-experience-is-much-less-happy-63161.

Staley, K. (2017). Changing what researchers 'think and do': Is this how engagement impacts on research? *Research for All, 1*, 158–67.

Stommel, J. (2018, 11 March). How to ungrade. *Jesse Stommel Blog site*. https://www.jessestommel.com/how-to-ungrade/.

Stray, C. (2021, 31 May-1 June). *The end of eternity: A short history of long classics*. [Conference presentation]. *Class and classics: Historiography, reception, challenges. Towards a democratisation of classical studies.* Gramsci Research Network.

Strolonga, P. (2014). Teaching uncomfortable subjects: When religious beliefs get in the way. In N.S. Rabinowitz & F. McHardy (eds.)(pp. 107–18).

Study International (2019, 5 December). PISA 2018 results show that youth reading skills must improve worldwide. *Study International.* https://www.studyinternational.com/news/pisa-2018-reading-skills-improve-worldwide/.

Sussman, L. (1978). The decline of basic skills: A suggestion so old that it's new. *Classical Journal, 73,* 351.

Sutton Trust (2019). *Elitist Britain 2019. The educational background of Britain's leading people.* The Sutton Trust & Social Mobility Commission.

Taylor, R. (2021, 7 December). Preparing our classroom communities for difficult conversations. *Brighter Thinking Blog.* https://www.cambridge.org/be/education/blog/2021/12/07/preparing-our-classroom-communities-for-difficult-conversations/.

TIMSS & PIRLS International Study Center. (2016). What makes a good reader: International findings from PIRLS 2016. TIMSS & PIRLS International Study Center. http://timssandpirls.bc.edu/pirls2016/international-results/pirls/summary/.

Trentman, E., McGregor, J. (2021). Introducing the special issue. *Critical Multilingualism Studies, 9*(1), 1–4.

Truijens, A. (2022, 14 April). Wat is het belang van het gymnasium? *De Volkskrant.* https://www.volkskrant.nl/cultuur-media/wat-is-het-belang-van-het-gymnasium-drie-boeken-geven-stof-tot-nadenken~b2007489.

UNDP, Oxford Poverty and Human Development Initiative. (2020). *Charting pathways out of multidimensional poverty.* United Nationals Development Programme.

UNICEF. (2021, December). *Preventing a lost decade.* UNICEF. https://www.unicef.org/media/112841/file/UNICEF%2075%20report.pdf.

Valcke, M. (2014). *Krachtige leeromgevingen.* Academia Press.

Valcke, M., De Craene, B. (2020). *Klasmanagement en reflectie: Omgaan met diversiteit in de klas,* 4th edition. Academia Press.

Valcke, M., Standaert, R. (2020). *Onderwijsbeleid in Vlaanderen,* 2nd edition. Acco.

Van Avermaet, P. et al. (2015). *MARS: Meertaligheid als realiteit op school.* Vlaams Ministerie van Onderwijs en Vorming.

van den Bergh, L. et al. (2010). The implicit prejudiced attitudes of teachers: Relations to teacher expectations and the ethnic achievement gap. *American Educational Research Journal, 47*(2), 497–527.

Van Praag, L. et al. (2019). Belgium: Cultural versus class explanations for ethnic inequalities in education in the Flemish and French communities. In P. Stevens, A.G. Dworkin (eds.), *The Palgrave handbook of race and ethnic inequalities in education* (pp. 159–213). Palgrave.

Vanderstichele, S. (2020, 17 September). Hoe een witte en een gekleurde school in Schaarbeek enkel de voordeur delen. *Bruzz.* https://www.bruzz.

be/onderwijs/hoe-een-witte-en-een-gekleurde-school-schaarbeek-enkel-de-voordeur-delen-2020-09-17.

Vantieghem, W. (2016). *Diversiteitsbarometer onderwijs – Vlaamse gemeenschap. Technisch rapport post 1: analytische review van het onderzoek naar ongelijkheden in het onderwijs.* Unia.

Vanwynsberghe, G. (2017). *Do schools and teachers leave their mark? Studies on long-term effects of schools and teachers on student outcomes* [doctoral dissertation]. KU Leuven.

Vasunia, P. (2013). *The classics and colonial India.* Oxford University Press.

Vidal Rodeiro, C., Zanini, N. (2015). The role of the A* grade at A level as a predictor of university performance in the United Kingdom. *Oxford Review of Education, 41*(5), 647–70.

Wagner, M., Perugini, D., Byram, M. (eds.) (2017). *Teaching intercultural competence across the age range: From theory to practice.* Multilingual Matters.

Walsh, L. (2016, 11 July). Giving it up in the classroom: Feminist classics and the burden of authority. *Eidolon.* https://eidolon.pub/giving-it-up-in-the-classroom-14c1afcfd69.

Wardle, M. (2021, 4 May). Languages in outstanding primary schools. *Education Inspection.* https://educationinspection.blog.gov.uk/2021/05/04/languages-in-outstanding-primary-schools/.

Welsh Government (2021, 25 March). Relative income poverty: April 2019 to March 2020. *Welsh Government.* https://gov.wales/relative-income-poverty-april-2019-march-2020-html.

Wesselmann, K. (2021). Chance Mehrsprachigkeit: Latein als sozialer Katalysator. *Zeitschrift für Interkulturellen Fremdsprachenunterricht, 26*(2), 251–71.

Wiggins, G.P., McTighe, J. (2005). *Understanding by Design,* 2nd edition. Association for Supervision and Curriculum Development.

Woolard, K.A. (2020). Language ideology. In J. Stanlaw (ed.), *The international encyclopedia of linguistic anthropology* (pp. 1–21). Wiley online.

Wyles, R., Hall, E. (eds.) (2016). *Women classical scholars: Unsealing the fountain from the Renaissance to Jacqueline de Romilly.* Oxford University Press.

Index

Printed in the United States
by Baker & Taylor Publisher Services